For Andrew,
my son and best friend

Contents

Preface

Conventions used in this Book

Text in a **Bold** style signifies an AutoCAD command or dialogue box text to be either accessed through the keyboard, screen icons or pull-down menus e.g. **DRAW/Line**.

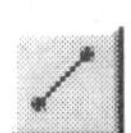

Icons used as paragraph starters and inline indicate that the command and/or selection can be accessed through that button.

The intended audience

No knowledge is assumed prior to this course of study. However, keyboard competence would be an advantage.

This book may be used to prepare for:-

The *City & Guilds Certificate in Two-Dimensional Computer-Aided Design Level 3, Course No. 4351/01* from September 1999.

The OCR Cambridge Certificate in Information Technology Computer Draughting Module No. 115.

A book entitled *Two-Dimensional CAD, City & Guilds 4351-01 Level 3 for AutoCAD 2000, Completed Examination Papers* by J T Roberts, containing solutions to the exercises is available from the publisher.

I have estimated the delivery time of this course to be approximately 20-30 hours excluding an introductory session where the very basics would be discussed.

The methods described in this book are not meant to be prescriptive and definitive. They are the way in which I approached the problems. Any improvements, corrections, omissions and/or constructive criticism would be gratefully accepted.

Please contact me at my e-mail address:-

jeff.roberts@nptc.ac.uk.

Jeff Roberts

Introduction

What is AutoCAD?

AutoCAD is a draughting and design software package which was first sold in 1982 under the name MicroCAD and ran under the CP/M operating system, which was popular before the days of MS-DOS. From those early days, AutoCAD has undergone many improvements and changes and today it is translated into 18 languages and used by millions of users worldwide.

Who is AutoCAD for?

Quite simply, if anything needs to be drawn then AutoCAD can be used to do it. Apart from an artist's sketching (and even here the boundaries are becoming more and more blurred with each release of AutoCAD) there is very little for which AutoCAD cannot be used. Architectural drawings, mechanical assemblies, transportation, retail space modelling, aeronautic and marine design, cartography, assembly line production diagrams and residential design are but a few examples where AutoCAD is used extensively. In addition, the availability of a plethora of third-party software packages which 'bolt-on' and work from within AutoCAD make it the designers' dream.

What if I use an earlier version of AutoCAD?

If you use AutoCAD R13 or an earlier version then this book will help you to update your skills very quickly by showing the 'icon' short-cuts. If you use AutoCAD R14 then the new wording that AutoCAD 2000 uses in its command-line sequences is used throughout the book and will get you up to speed in the minimum of time.

I've never drawn in 3D

If you have never drawn in 3D, used Model Space and Paper Space or created a new UCS the book introduces these in easy to follow instructions.

Many existing users of AutoCAD are confused by Paper Space and moving the UCS icon to a new drawing plane. The book approaches these topics on a step-by-step basis so that you can gain the necessary skills and confidence as you progress.

What's in the book?

The book approaches the problem of learning AutoCAD 2000 from a new angle - a scenario is developed in the form of a fictitious building, starting from a blank electronic drawing sheet and ending with a 3D building. The final drawing shows 3 different views placed on a border with drawing titling etc.
It has been developed in this way to simulate, as closely as possible, how the drawing would be approached in a live situation. At the end of this book you should have gained the skills and confidence to attempt quite complex drawings.

The Scenario

The scenario drawing is the fictitious administrative headquarters of a small electronics company. The drawing is developed from a blank screen — in much the same way that you would start any drawing. The drawing is carried out in 2D, with walls, doors and windows being constructed for the internal detail and landscaping features such as a paved patio, pond, driveway and boundary wall added externally.
Reusable symbols are created in the form of the furniture. The drawing is dimensioned and textual data added as annotations.
Finally, the drawing is converted from 2D to 3D and a tiled, pitched roof is added. Three views of the drawing are created on a drawing border, the drawing title details are added and lastly, the drawing is plotted.

Chapter 1 — The Basics

Activate AutoCAD

To Activate AutoCAD

- Click on **Start**, **Programs** and **AutoCAD 2000** as shown in Fig. 1.1.

Your Windows setup may be different but you should have a similar layout to that shown in Figure 1.1.

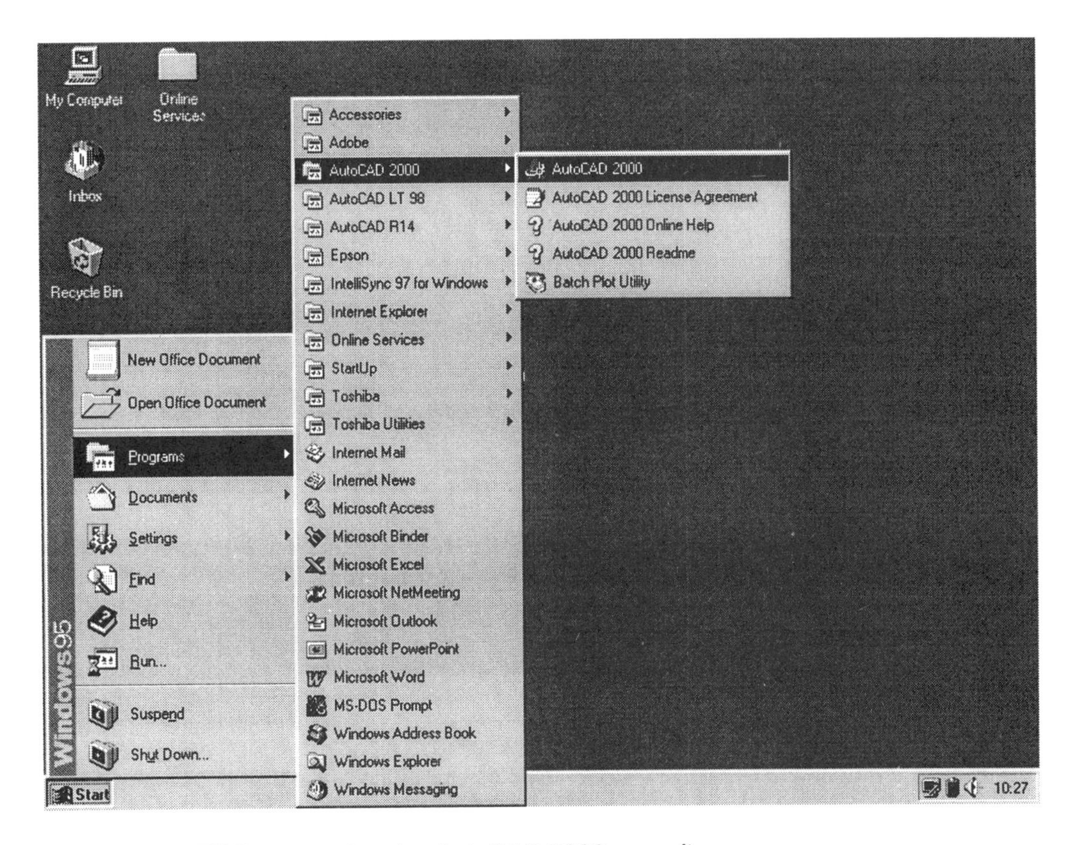

Figure 1.1. Windows NT/95 screen showing AutoCAD 2000 menu item

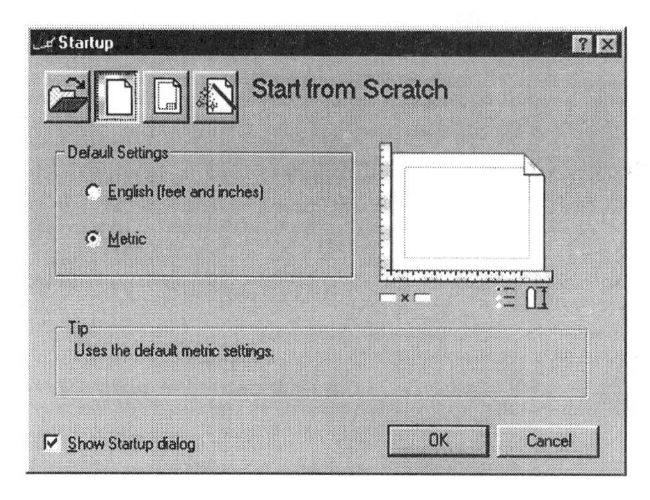

Figure 1.2. *Startup dialogue box*

Once you have activated AutoCAD the **Startup** dialogue box appears as shown in Figure 1.2. Select the '**Start from Scratch**' button and **Metric** option if not already selected. This will present you with the drawing screen and editor as shown in Figure 1.3. Your screen should look similar to Figure 1.3 but you may have more or different toolbars visible. When we start the target drawing we will use the '**Wizard**' option to set up the drawing unit type and drawing area size.

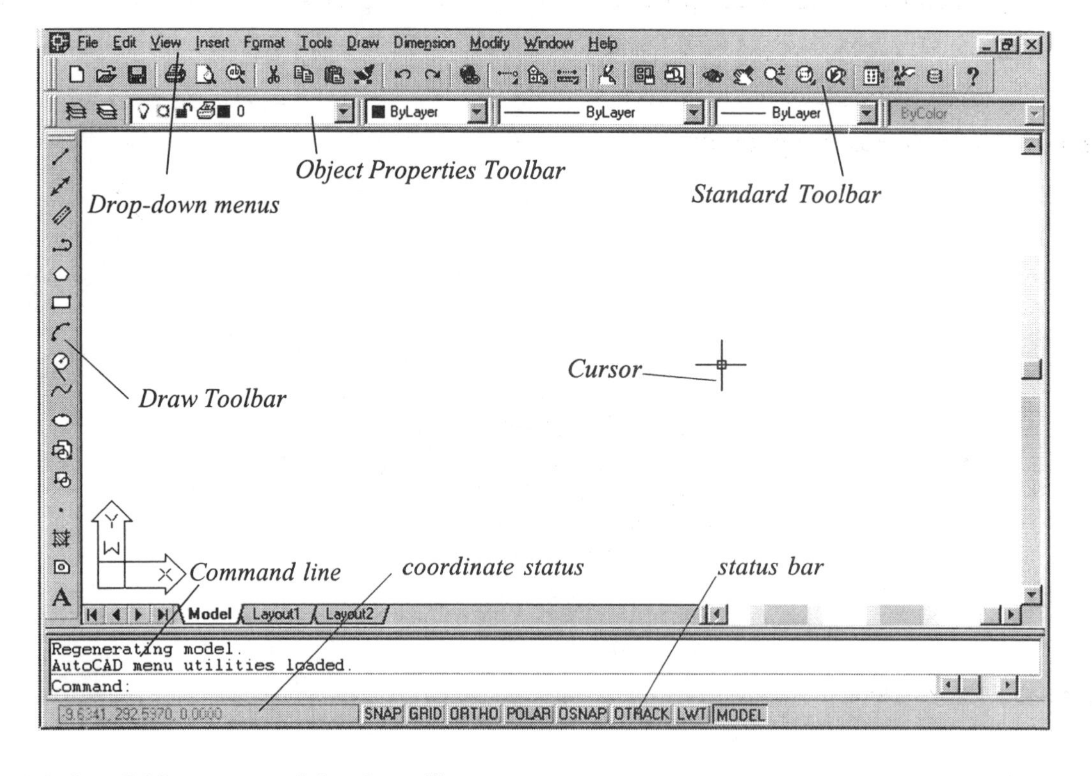

Figure 1.3. *AutoCAD screen and drawing editor*

The Keyboard

AutoCAD has special uses for certain parts of the keyboard. The keys prefixed with the letter ‘F’ (F1-F12) are called Function keys or are sometimes known as ‘hot’ keys and their uses are listed below.

F1 AutoCAD Help
F2 Toggle between graphics window and command window
F3 Running object snap on/off
F5 Cycle through isometric planes
F6 Cycle through coordinate display types
F7 Grid mode on/off
F8 Orthographic mode on/off
F9 Snap mode on/off
F10 Polar mode on/off
F11 Object Tracking Mode

The other keys that have special uses are:-

Esc Cancels the last operation
Spacebar Acts as the Enter key when in drawing mode (inserts a space in text mode)
< Used when specifying polar coordinates and any figure following the < is an angle
@ Used when specifying relative and polar coordinates and translates as ‘in relation to the last position of the cursor’
Enter Completes an operation

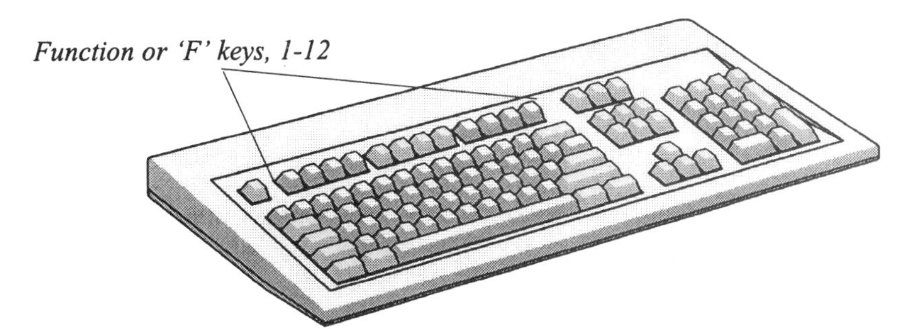

Figure 1.4. *The keyboard*

The Pointing Device

Pointing can be either done with a mouse or a digitising tablet and AutoCAD can be set up to accept both methods.

The mouse can be either a 2 or 3 button model as shown in Figure 1.5 and normally the left button is the 'pick' or select button. The right button is the equivalent of **Enter** on the keyboard and activates a floating dialogue box where **Enter** is chosen to complete an operation. The middle button on a 3 button mouse can be programmed for almost any AutoCAD function but is outside the scope of this book.

Similarly, digitising tablet puck buttons can be programmed for almost any function, but in both cases only the 'pick' button cannot be re-allocated.

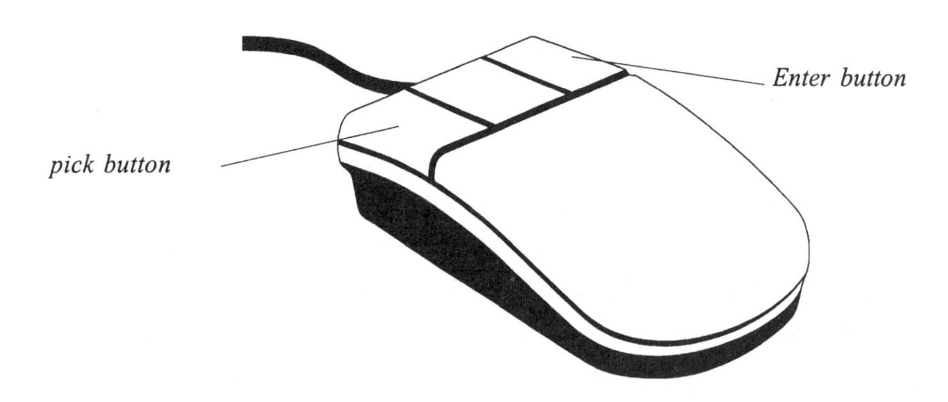

***Figure 1.5**. The mouse*

Figure 1.6 shows the digitising tablet overlay which is supplied with AutoCAD and is stuck down on the digitising tablet and allows picking of operations. Since the advent of Windows the digitising tablet has decreased in popularity and has been superseded by the mouse.

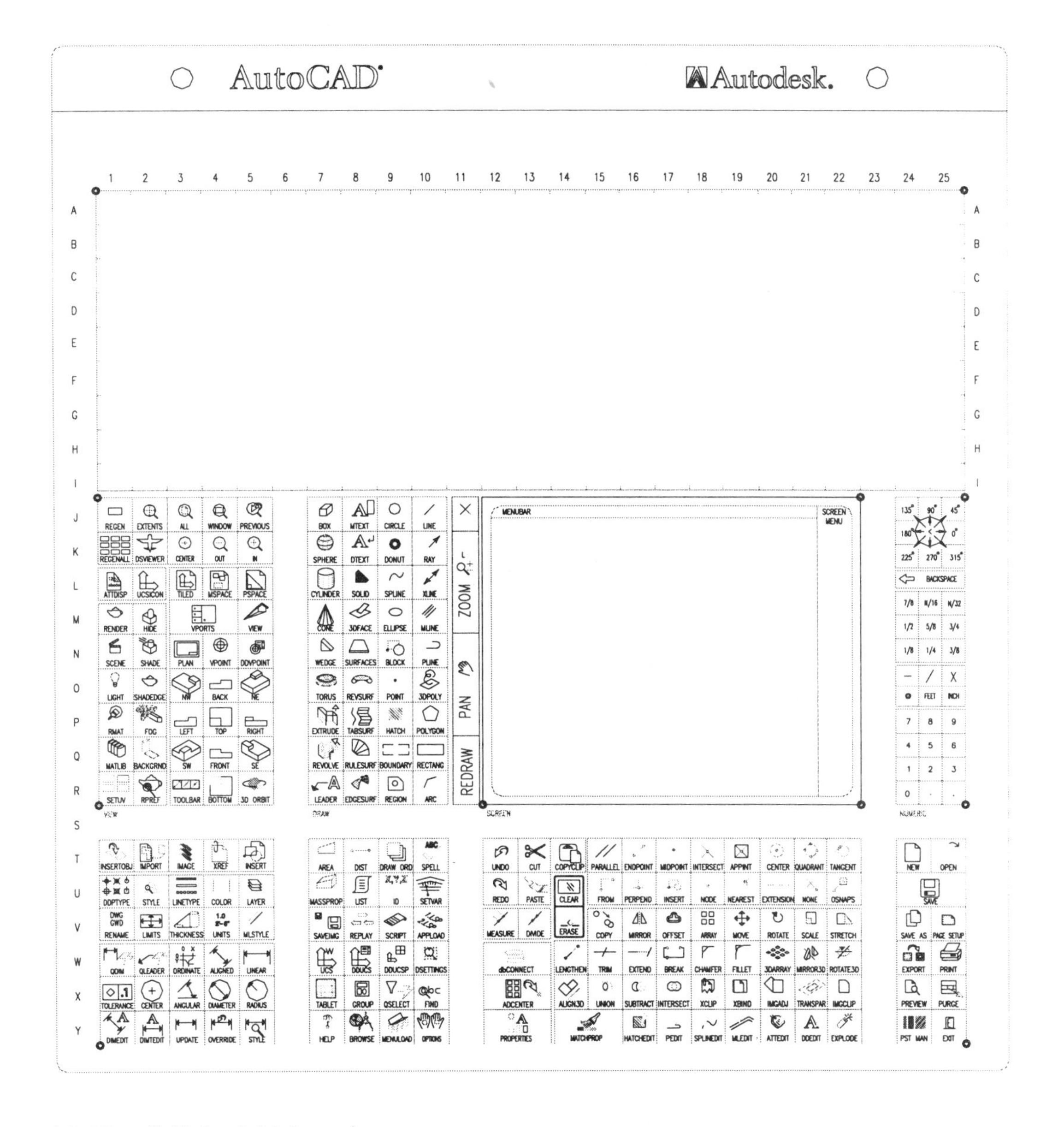

***Figure 1.6**. The digitising tablet overlay*

The Text Window

The text window is similar to the command window in which you enter commands and view prompts and messages. Unlike the command window, the text window contains a complete command history for the current AutoCAD session. You can use the text window to view lengthy output of commands such as **List**, which displays detailed information about objects you select.

To display the text window while you are in the graphics area, press **F2**. The text window is displayed in front of the graphics area as shown in Figure 1.7. If you press **F2** while in the text window, the graphics area is redisplayed. If either the graphics area or the text window has been minimized, press **F2** to display it at its last configured size. The **F2** key functions as a toggle only if both the graphics window and the text window are open.

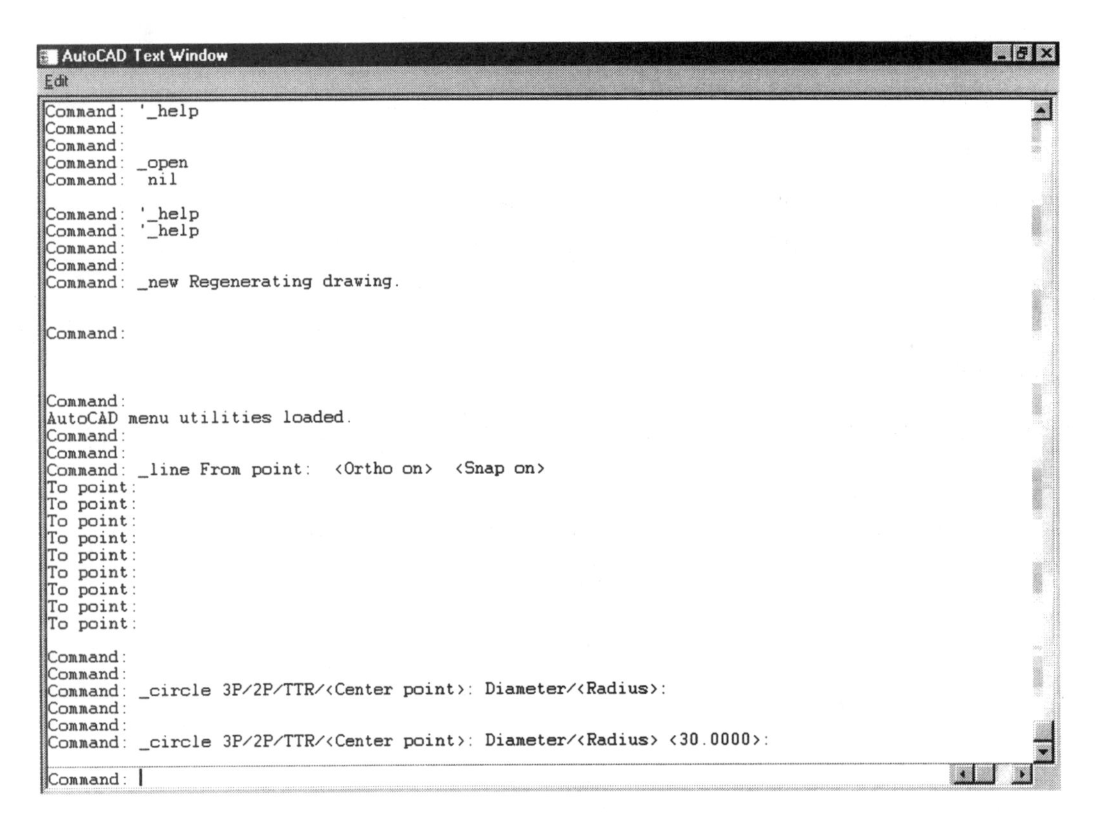

***Figure 1.7**. The AutoCAD text window*

Drawing in AutoCAD

You can draw in any one of many methods in AutoCAD, and in any combination. Listed below are the methods which we shall use.

Absolute Coordinates

With the bottom left hand corner of the drawing area being 0 in the X coordinate direction, and 0 in the Y coordinate direction you can specify coordinates in relation to that datum base point. Absolute coordinates are always entered as x,y in that order. e.g.

20,30

would specify a distance of 20 along the X axis (horizontally) and 30 along the Y axis (vertically) as shown in Figure 1.9.

Relative Coordinates

Relative coordinates specify a position in the X and Y axis in relation to the current position. e.g.

@100,0

would move the cursor to a point relative to the current position by 100 in the X axis and 0 in the Y axis. Note that relative coordinates are always preceded with the '@' sign and the format of x,y as shown in Figure 1.9.

Polar Coordinates

AutoCAD measures angles in an anti-clockwise direction with 0° at the 3 o'clock position as shown in Figure 1.8.
Polar coordinates are a combination of distance and angle in relation to the current position. e.g.

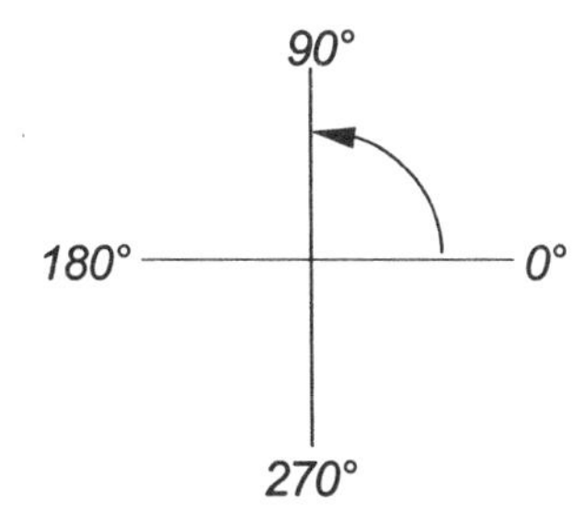

***Figure 1.8**. AutoCAD method of measuring angles*

@50<45

would produce a line with a length of 50 units at an angle of 45°. It uses a combination of relative coordinates with the '@' sign preceding the distance followed by the '<' sign to signify that what follows is an angle.

Figure 1.9 shows the combinations of absolute, relative and polar coordinate entry.

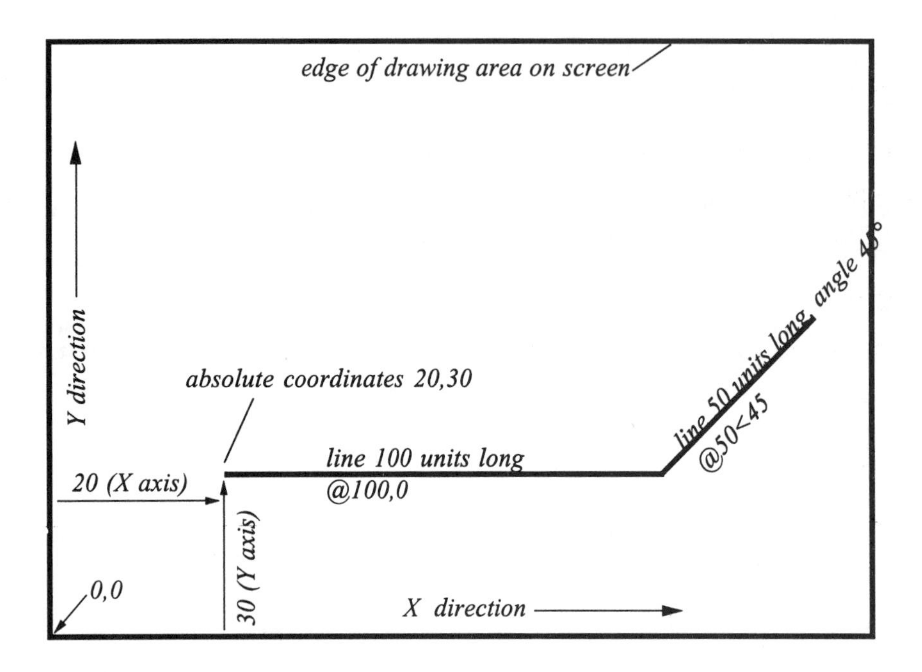

***Figure 1.9**. Coordinate combinations*

Chapter 2 — Setting up the Drawing

Target Drawing

The target drawing is shown in Figure 2.1 and is the fictitious headquarters of a small electronics company. We will build this drawing up as shown in Figure 2.1 and continue to produce a 3D drawing as shown in Figures 2.2 and 2.3. Lastly we will produce 3 different views of the drawing on a single sheet of paper with a pre-drawn border as in Figure 2.4.

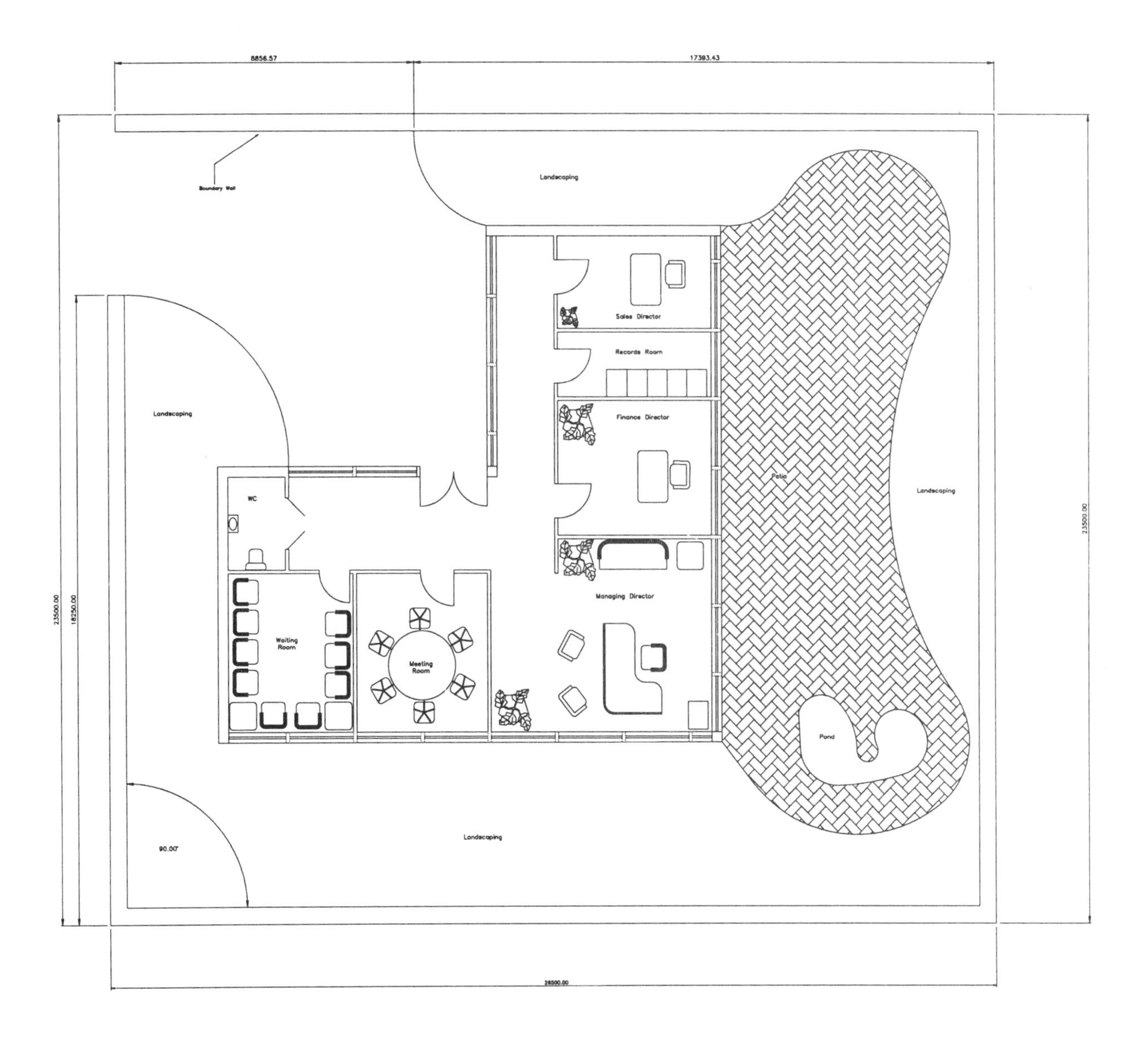

***Figure 2.1**. The 2D plan target drawing*

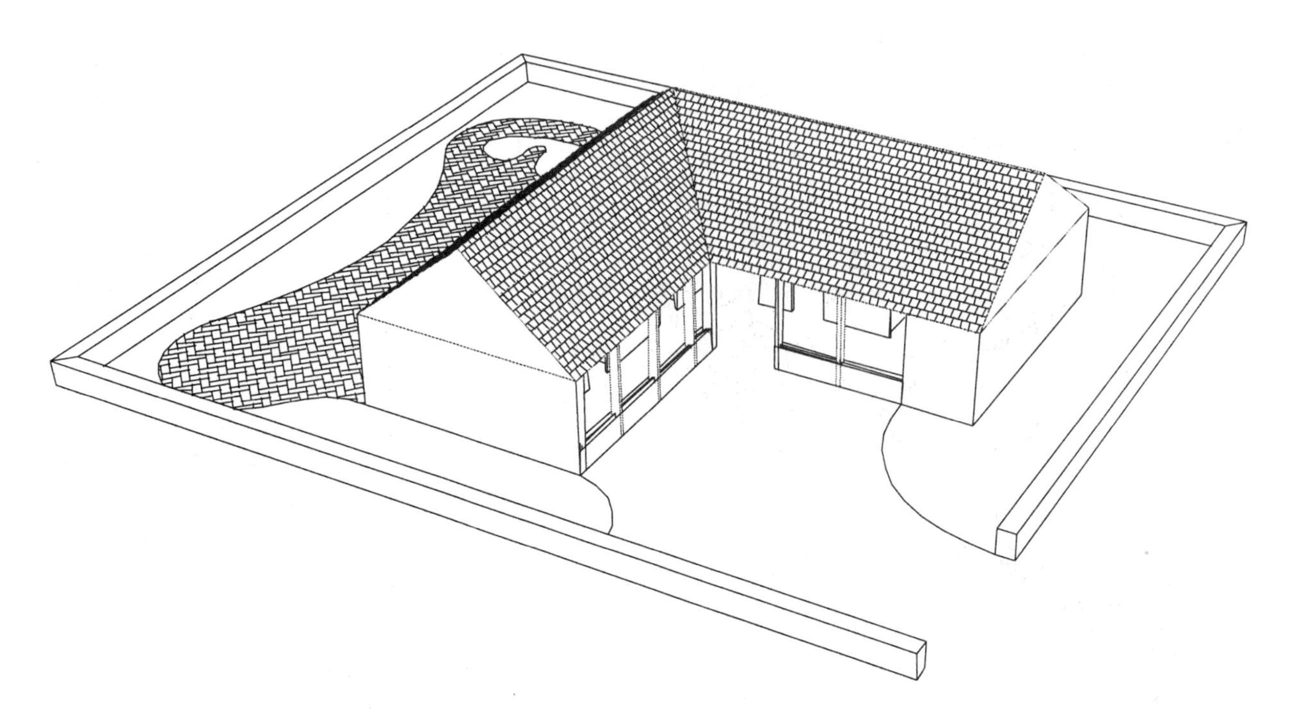

***Figure 2.2**. A view of the 3D model with the roof added and a height given to the boundary wall*

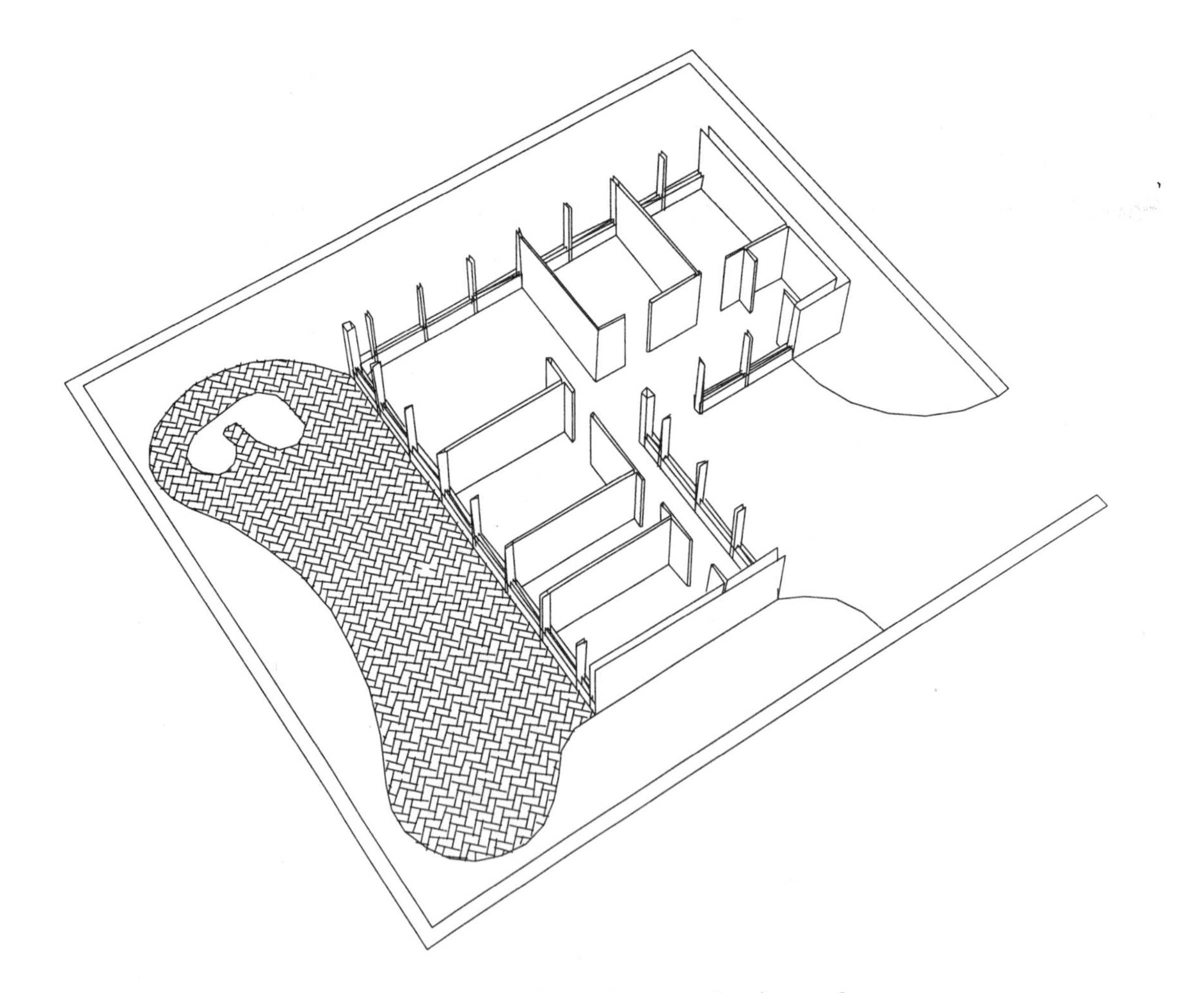

***Figure 2.3**. A different 3D view with the roof, text, dimension and other layers frozen.*

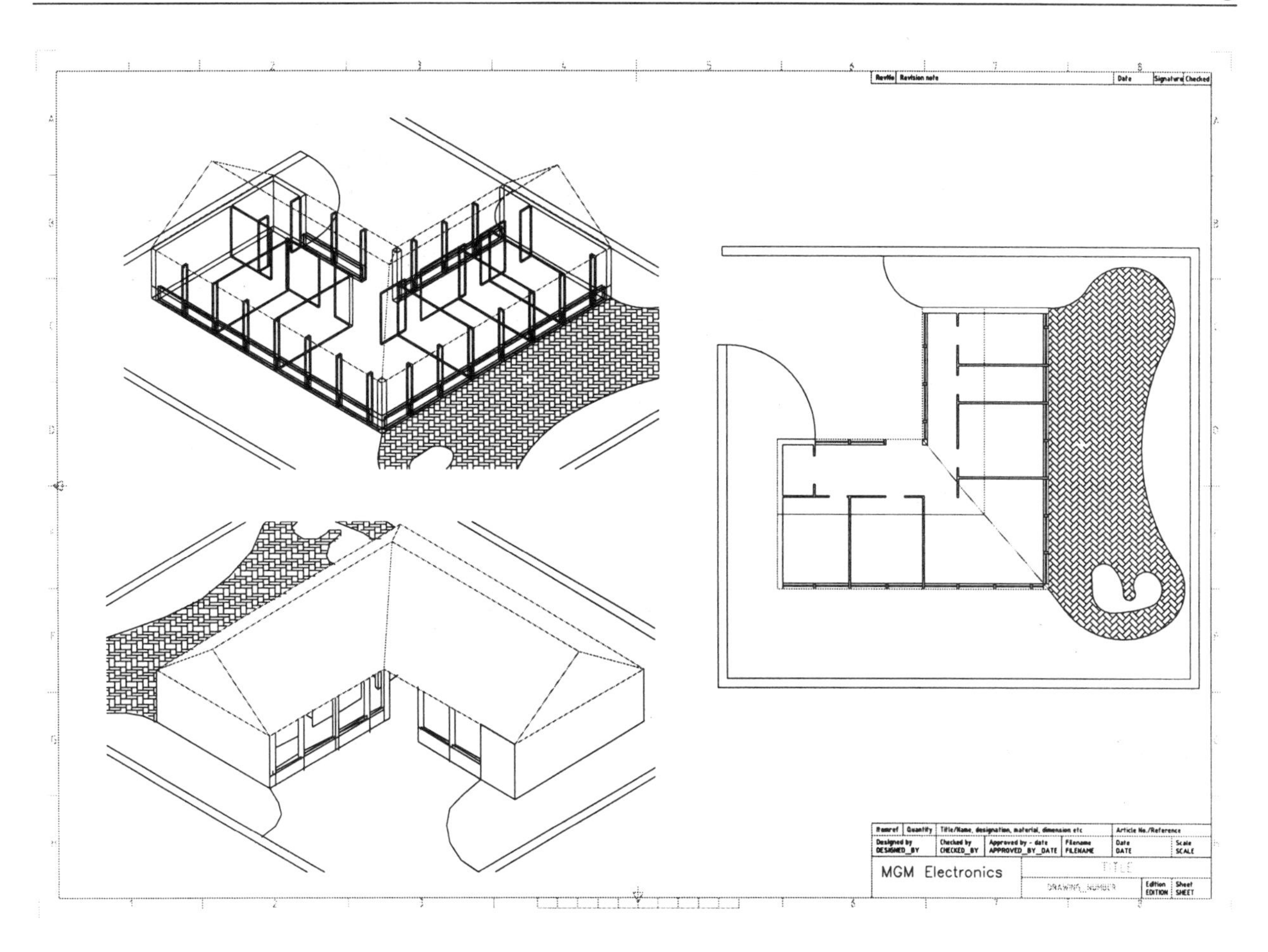

***Figure 2.4**. 3 different views of the building on one drawing with border information*

Starting the Target Drawing

We will now start the drawing as shown in Figure 2.1. If you have activated AutoCAD already as described on page 5, click on the drop-down menu **Files/Exit** and AutoCAD will close down.

- Activate AutoCAD as shown in Figures 1.1 and 1.2 but this time click on **Use a Wizard** as shown in Figure 2.5. This sets the units of measurement and the drawing area size.
- Click on **Quick Setup**.
- Click on **OK**.

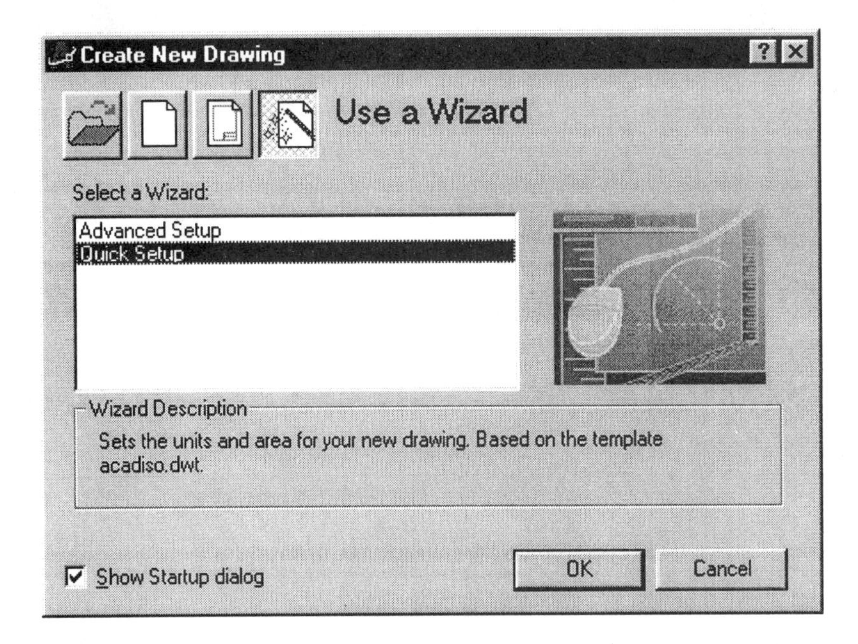

***Figure 2.5**. Create New Drawing dialogue box*

The first **Quick Setup** dialogue box appears as shown in Figure 2.6 which sets the unit of measurement.

- Click on the **Decimal** radio button to set decimal units.
- Click on the **Next** button.

The second **Quick Setup** dialogue box appears as shown in Figure 2.6 which sets the drawing area or limits.

- In the **Width** box enter **30000** and in the **Length** box enter **25000** as shown in Figure 2.6. The drawing area must be bigger than the full size of the building as AutoCAD draws in full size on screen. Any scaling of the drawing is done at plotting time.
- Click on **Finish**.

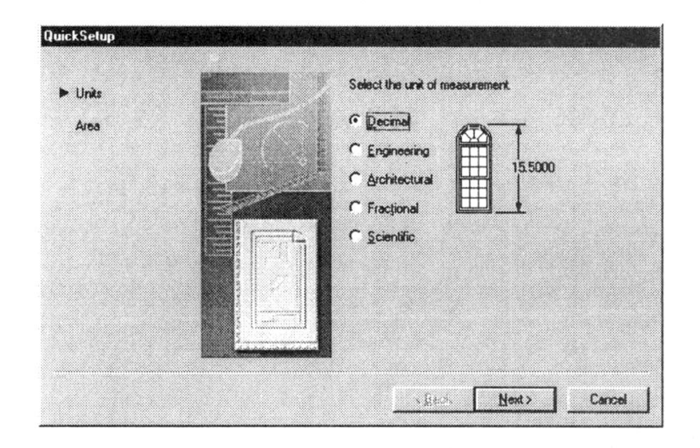

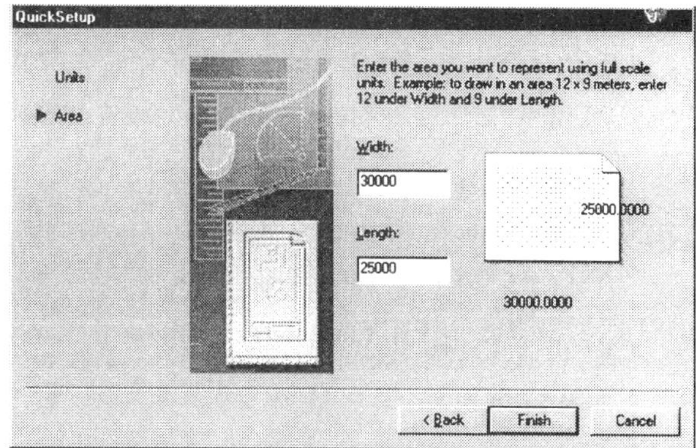

***Figure 2.6**. Quick Setup windows for setting unit type and drawing area*

The drawing screen will appear as shown in Figure 1.3. Whilst we have changed the size of the drawing area AutoCAD still only shows the default sheet size, i.e. a portion of the drawing in the lower left corner. To prove this, move your cursor to the upper right hand corner of the screen and read the x,y coordinate values. They should be close to the default values of **420**, **297**.

We must now show all of the drawing area on screen. We do this by using the **Zoom/All** command. At the command line type the text shown in bold text, pressing **Enter** after each entry.

> *Command:* ***zoom***
> *All/Center/Dynamic/Extents/Previous/Scale(X/XP)/Window/<Realtime>:* ***a***

AutoCAD will now regenerate the screen to show the whole of the drawing area. Move your cursor once again to the top right corner of the screen and the x,y values should now be close to **30000**, **25000**.

Drawing Aids

To enable drawing at speed, AutoCAD assists us with tools that aid data entry. We will now set up a screen grid of dots and a cursor snap value that allows the cursor to 'jump' incrementally in coincidence with the grid value. We can change the grid value and also make the snap value non-coincident to the grid at any time.

- From the pull-down menu use **Tools/Drafting Settings** and a dialogue box will appear as shown in Figure 2.7.
- Change the **X** spacing values for **Snap** to **100**.
- Change the **X** spacing values for **Grid** to **1000**.
- Turn **Snap** and **Grid** on by clicking in the **Snap On** and **Grid On** boxes.

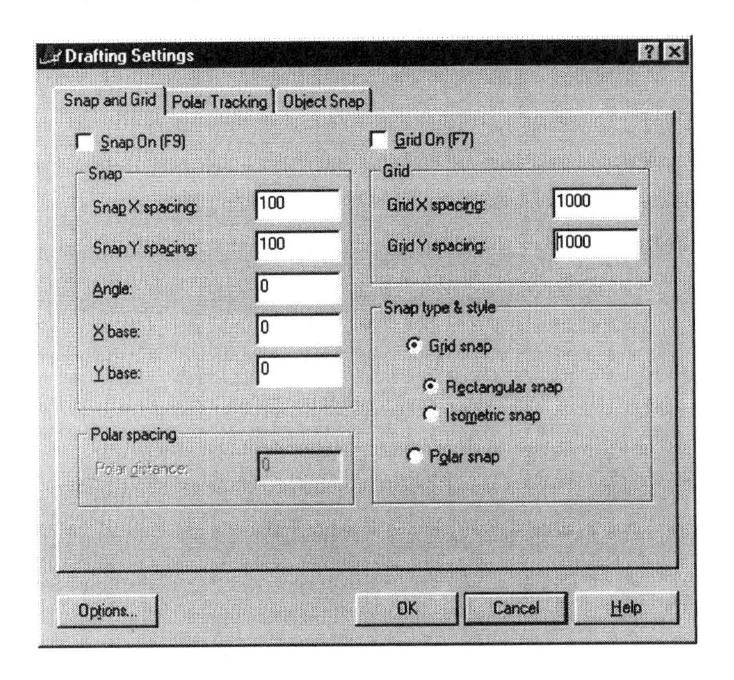

Figure 2.7. Drafting Settings dialogue box

- Click on **OK**.

You do not need to change the **Y** spacing values as **X** and **Y** are the same and clicking **OK** automatically enters the **X** value into the **Y** value. If you wanted a rectangular grid, for instance, you would change the **Y** value before clicking **OK**. Figure 2.7 shows the **Drafting Settings** dialogue box with the values changed.

Units Precision

Even though we used the **Wizard** to set up the type of unit to decimal input, we were not able to set up the precision of the input i.e. to how many places of decimal we need to be accurate. On distances the nearest millimetre is adequate for this type of design.

- From the pull-down menu select **Format/Units** and change the precision to 3 decimal places and 0 for angles as shown in Figure 2.8.

If you reactivate the **Drafting Settings** dialogue box, the **Snap** and **Grid X** and **Y** values are now accurate to three decimal places.

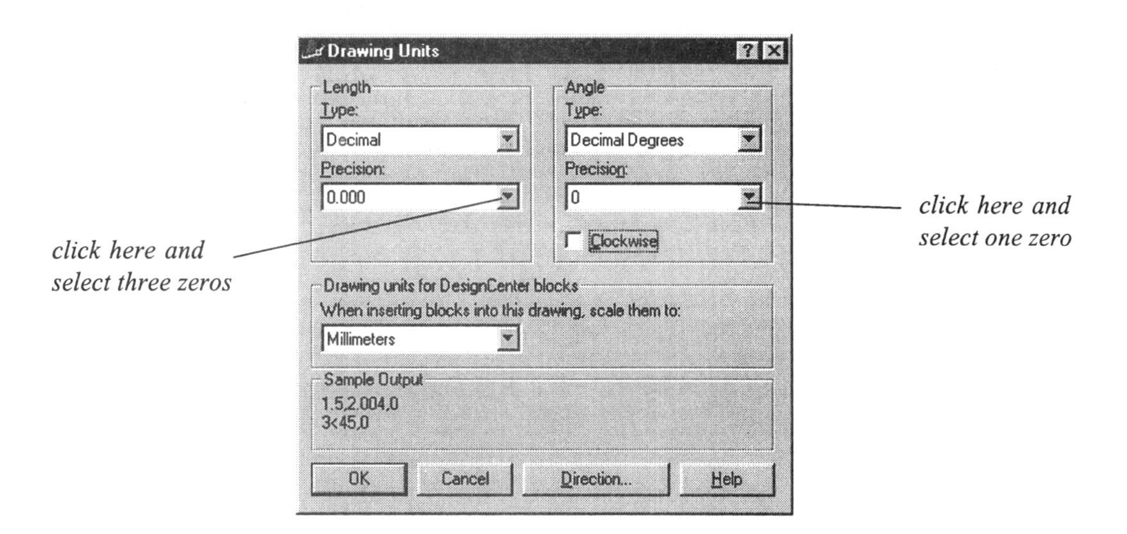

***Figure 2.8**. Drawing Units dialogue box*

Drawing using Layers

Layering a drawing in AutoCAD is similar to using overlays in manual draughting. For example, in our target drawing all the walls are drawn on one layer and the doors on another. The roof has its own layer allocated as does the roof tiling. At any time we can choose to 'hide' any of the layers so the objects drawn on that layer are not visible on screen. If objects are not visible on screen then they will not be plotted either. If you refer to Figures 2.3. and 2.4 you will see a good example of 'freezing' or hiding layers. Remember also, that **Layer 0** is created by AutoCAD as the default layer and should not be renamed. It is good practice to decide on your layers before you start drawing. It is probable that you will have to add layers as you proceed but do try to be methodical. Some of the layers for our target drawing are listed below.

Layer Name	Colour
Walls	Red
Doors	Cyan
Windows	Green
Roof	Blue
Patioedge	Yellow
Patiohatch	Magenta
Roofhatch	White
Boundary	Your Choice
Dimensions	Red
Furniture	Your Choice
Text	Cyan

To Add a New Layer

- Click on the **Layer** button in the **Object Properties** toolbar and the **Layer Properties Manager** dialogue box will appear as shown in Figure 2.9.
- Click on **New**.

A new layer will be added called **Layer1**.

- Type in the name of a layer. e.g. **Walls**, and the name **Layer1** will be replaced by layer **Walls**.
- Repeat this for all the required layers shown above.

As the drawing progresses, we will add further layers.

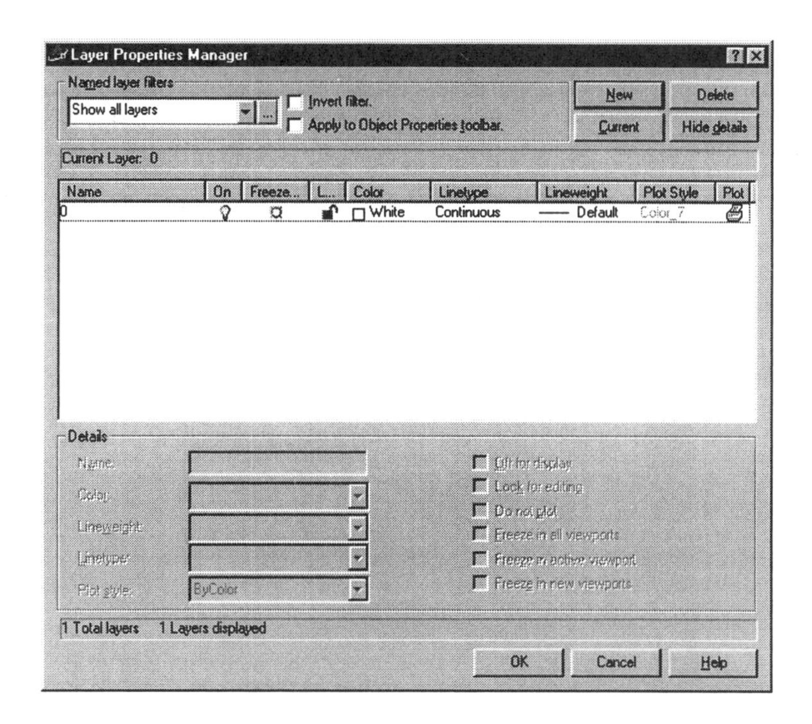

Figure 2.9 *Layer Property Manager dialogue box showing default layer 0*

Layer Colours

It is a good idea to give your layers different colours so that they become easily distinguishable on screen and when plotted.

To do this:-

- Click on the white rectangle under 'C' on the **Walls** layer as shown in Figure 2.10 and the **Select Color** dialogue box appears as shown in Figure 2.11.
- Select **'red'** from the **Standard Colours** palette.
- Click **OK**.

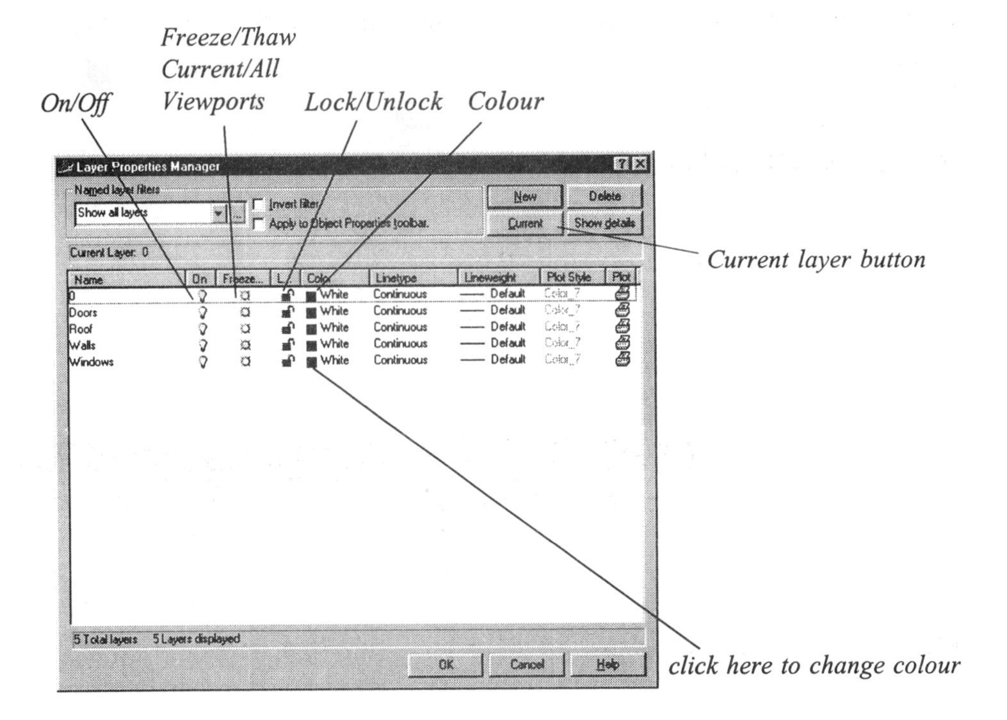

Figure 2.10. *Layer Property Manager dialogue box with some of the layers in place*

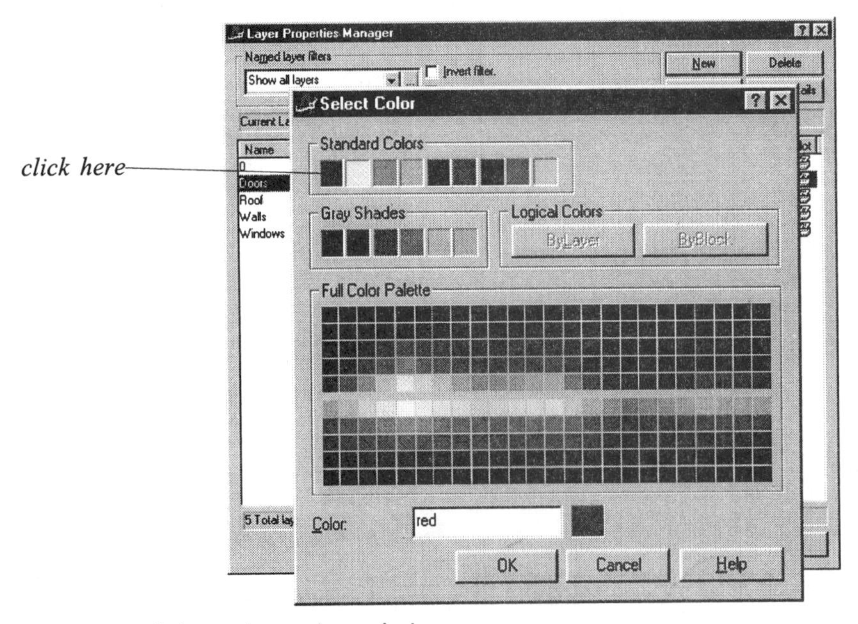

Figure 2.11. *Layer dialogue box colour window*

You will see that the **Walls** layer colour is now **red**.

- Repeat this operation for all of the layers giving them their colours as listed above.

When you have completed the colour changes:-

- Click on the **Walls** layer by clicking on the word '**Walls**' and select the **Current** button as shown in Figure 2.10.

This changes the layer currently being drawn on to the **Walls** layer in preparation for the building outline.

- Click **OK** to close the layers dialogue box.

The layer toolbar should now show the word **Walls** with the layer colour as shown in Figure 2.12.

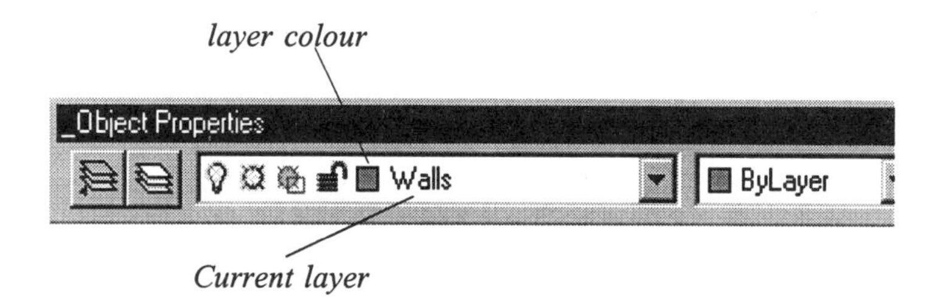

***Figure 2.12**. Object Properties Toolbar showing Current layer & Colour*

Saving Drawings

It is good practice to save your drawing every 10 minutes or so, as you proceed, rather than when you finish drawing.

- Click on the **QSave** button and the **Save Drawing As** dialogue box will appear as shown in Figure 2.13.

The drawing does not have a name yet and AutoCAD automatically inserts the filename as '**Drawing**'. Overtype the word '**Drawing**' with '**MGM Electronics**' and click on **OK**. If you are saving the drawing to the floppy drive click on the **Save in** pull-down menu and click on **3½ Floppy [A:]**.
The drawing is now saved up to this point. When you save your drawing for the first time the '**Save Drawing As**' dialogue box will appear but after that, clicking on the **QSave** button (quick save) does not produce a dialogue box but saves the drawing to disc.

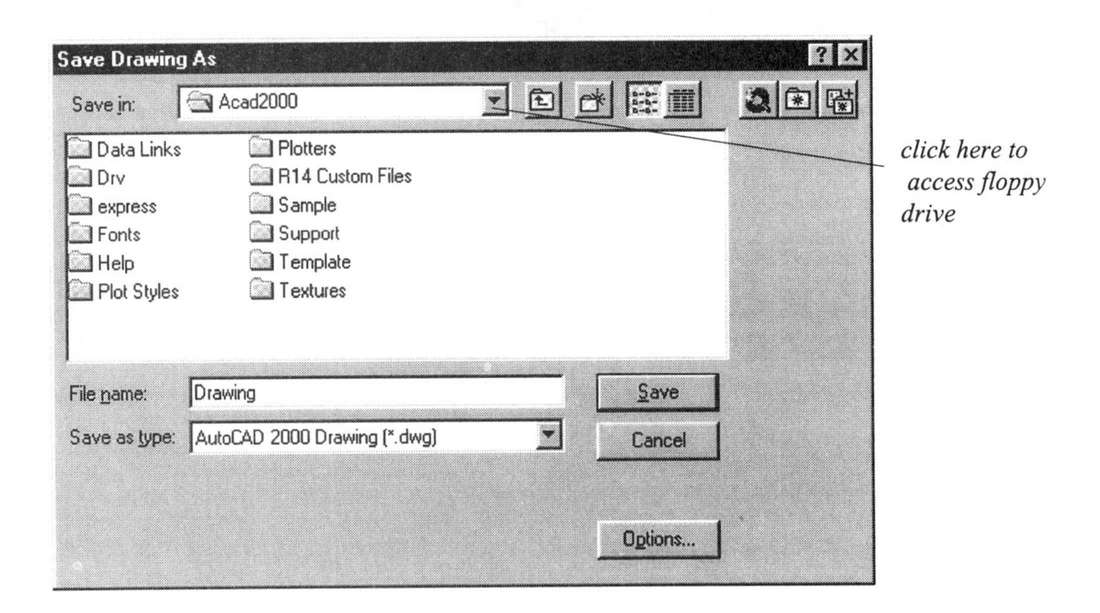

***Figure 2.13**. The Save Drawing as Dialogue box*

Chapter 3 — Drawing the Building

We will leave the grid visible but turn **Snap** off initially although it is not essential to do so. Can you remember how to toggle **Snap** off using the keyboard? Try **F9**.

We are now ready to design the headquarters of MGM Electronics.

We will use **Absolute coordinates** to draw the outline of the building as shown in Figure 3.1.

Drawing

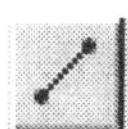

- Pick the line command from the **Draw** toolbar and type, at the Command line, the text shown in bold text only. Press **Enter** after each input.

Command: _line From point:	***5000,6000***
Specify next point:	***20000,6000***
Specify next point:	***20000,21000***
Specify next point:	***13000,21000***
Specify next point:	***13000,14000***
Specify next point:	***5000,14000***
Specify next point:	***5000,6000***
Specify next point:	***Enter***

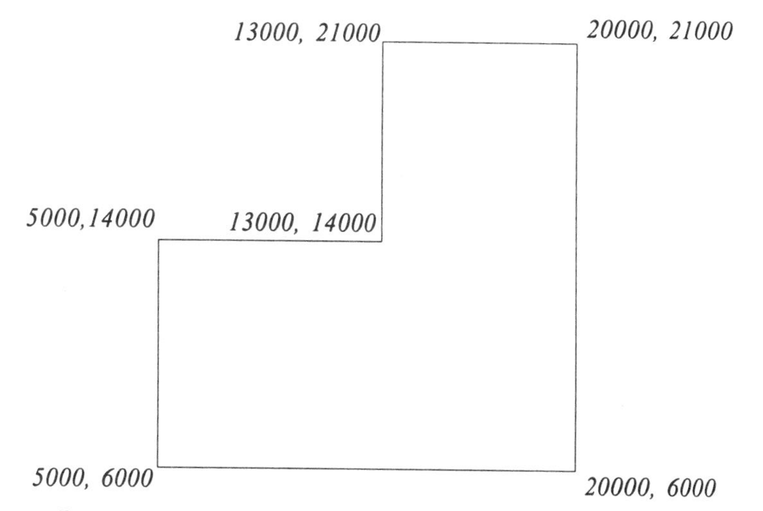

***Figure 3.1**. The Building outline*

Click on the **Undo** button at any time to retrace your steps if you make errors.

We will now draw the inner lines of the exterior wall as shown in Figure 3.2. The wall width is 300mm. Can you calculate what the absolute coordinates will be? If you are having difficulty the answer is below.

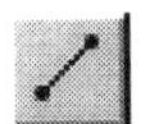

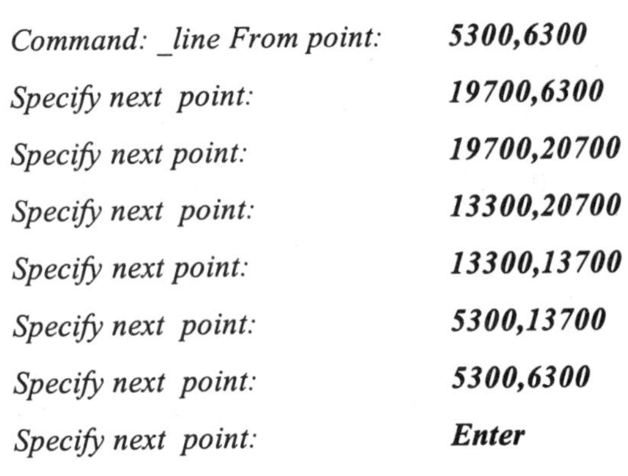

Command: _line From point:	***5300,6300***
Specify next point:	***19700,6300***
Specify next point:	***19700,20700***
Specify next point:	***13300,20700***
Specify next point:	***13300,13700***
Specify next point:	***5300,13700***
Specify next point:	***5300,6300***
Specify next point:	***Enter***

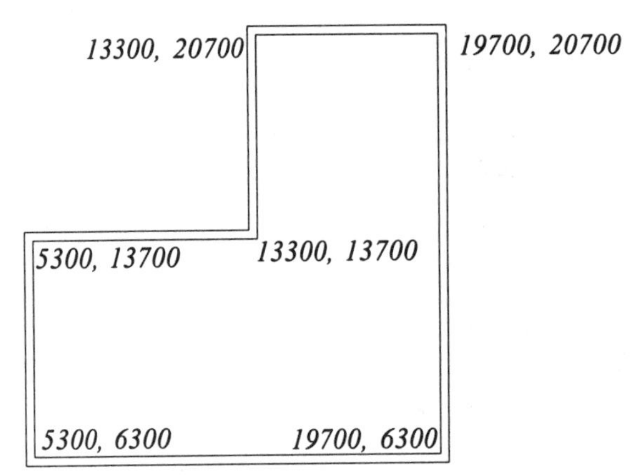

***Figure 3.2**. The Inner lines of the exterior wall*

For the inner partition walls we will draw with **Relative coordinates** but starting with an **Absolute coordinate** as shown in Figure 3.3.

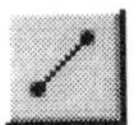

Command: _line From point:	***5000,11000***
Specify next point:	***@10000,0***
Specify next point:	***@0,9700***
Specify next point:	***Enter***

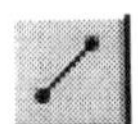

Command: _line From point:	***5000,10900***
Specify next point:	***@10100,0***
Specify next point:	***@0,9800***
Specify next point:	***Enter***

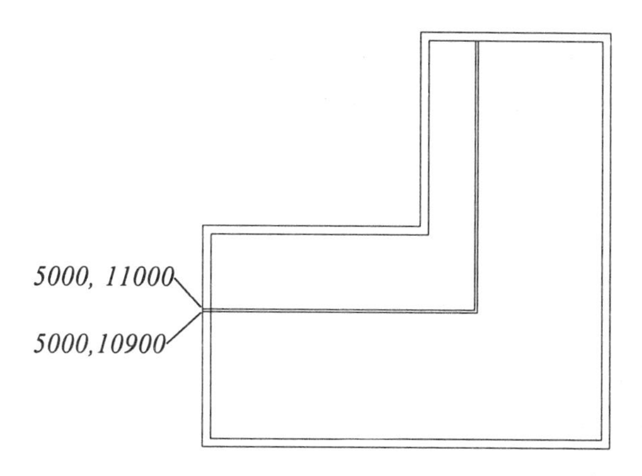

***Figure 3.3**. Drawing the partition walls*

Next, we will add the partitions separating the rooms again starting with an **Absolute coordinate** as shown in Figure 3.4.

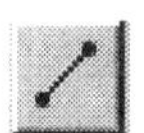

Command: _line From point:	***9000,6300***
Specify next point:	***@0,4600***
Specify next point:	***Enter***

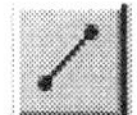

Command: _line From point:	***9100,6300***
Specify next point:	***@0,4600***
Specify next point:	***Enter***

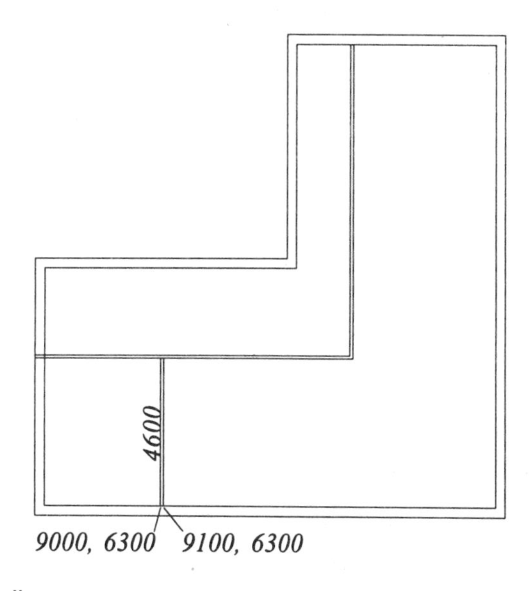

***Figure 3.4**. Internal Partition wall*

The remaining partitions are shown in Figure 3.5 starting with **Absolute coordinates**, room widths and lengths. Can you draw them by calculating the **Relative coordinates**? All of the partition widths are 100mm.

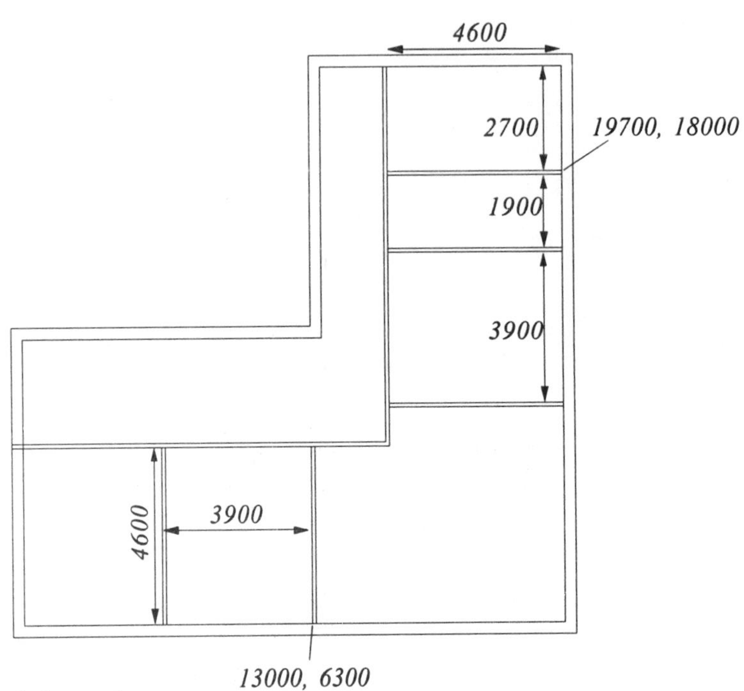

***Figure 3.5**. Partition wall dimensions*

Enlarging the view of the Drawing (The Zoom Command)

We now need to create the door openings which are 1000mm wide, except for the double doors. To create these accurately it is better for us to have an enlarged view of the drawing and move around the drawing in that view. AutoCAD provides a tool called **Zoom** which allows us to specify an area of the drawing on which we want to work.

You can use the **Zoom** command by selecting **View/Zoom** from the pull-down menu or with the **Zoom/ Window** button on the Toobar but we will load the **Zoom Toolbar** so that you become familiar with the process of loading toolbars.

- From the pull-down menu select **View/Toolbars** and the **Toolbars** dialogue box will appear as shown in Figure 3.6.
- Scroll down and place a check in the '**Zoom**' box and click on **Close**.

This will load the **Zoom** toolbar on your screen and is ready for use.

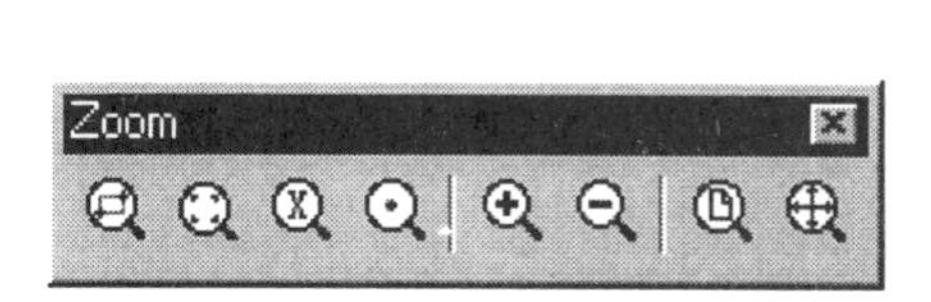

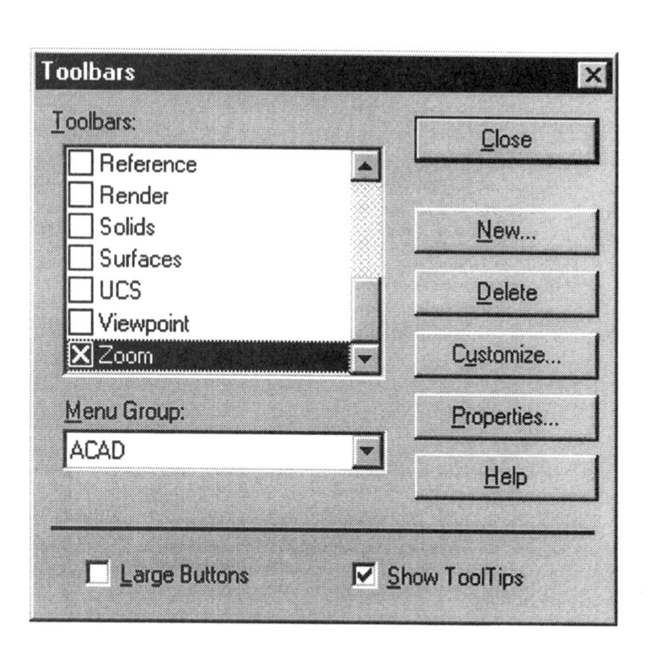

***Figure 3.6**. The Toolbars dialogue box and the loaded Zoom toolbar*

■ Click on **Zoom/Window** and form a rectangle with your cursor by picking two diagonally opposite corners of the rectangular area as shown in Figure 3.7. It is shown shaded here for clarity only. Figure 3.9 shows the new view of the drawing.

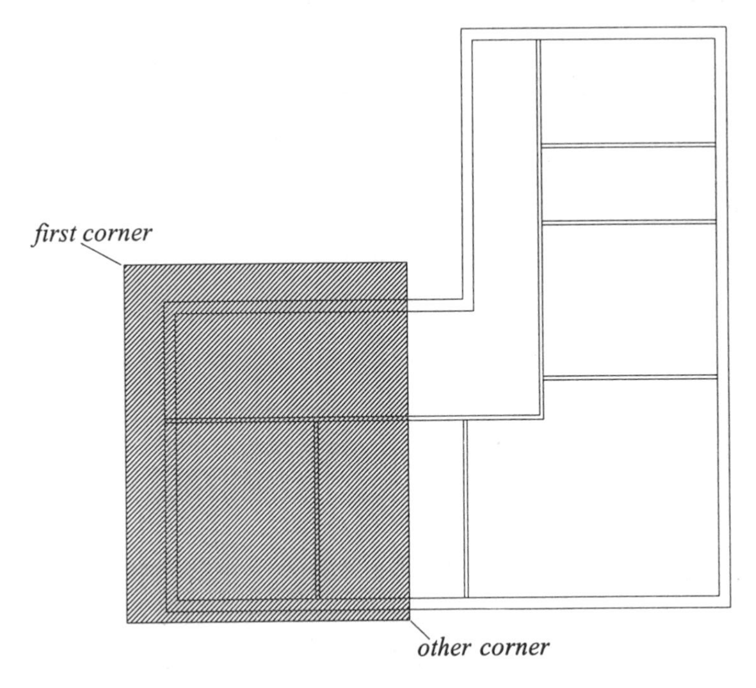

***Figure 3.7**. Zoom window area*

Modifying the Drawing

If you look at the enlarged view in Figure 3.9 you will see that the corridor partition lines overlap the left hand wall and touch the outer wall which is the way that we drew it. We need to correct this with the commands **Modify/Trim** and **Modify/Break**. We now need to load the **Modify** toolbar. Using the same method as we used for loading the **Zoom** toolbar, load the **Modify** toolbar (not **Modify II**) with **View/Toolbars**.

■ Select **View/Toolbars**.

■ Put a check in the **Modify** box.

■ Click on **Close**.

The toolbar will appear within your drawing area as shown in Figure 3.8 with the icons all on one line. You have the option of leaving it where it appears but it is more convenient to dock it to the left,right or top of the drawing area.

■ To move the toolbar click and drag it to its destination on a part of the toolbar outside of the button commands as shown in Figure 3.8. On the perimeter of the screen it will adopt the shape of the toolbar closest to it but the contents remain the same.

■ You can do the same for the **Zoom** toolbar also.

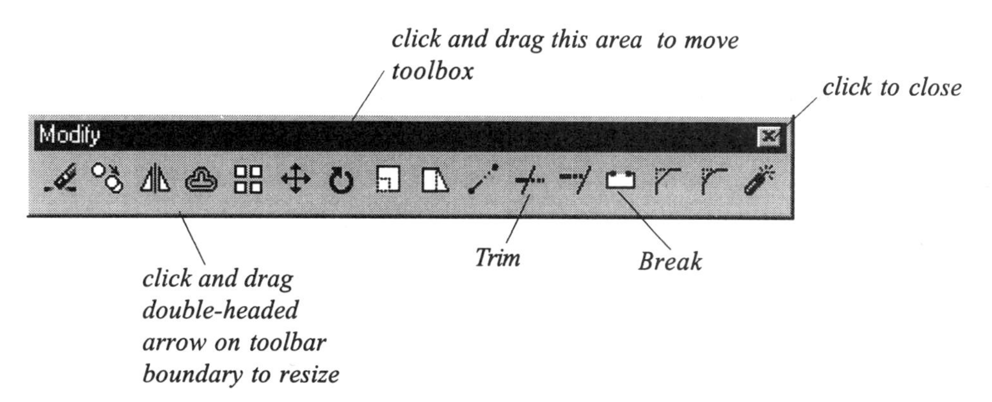

Figure 3.8. Toolbox properties

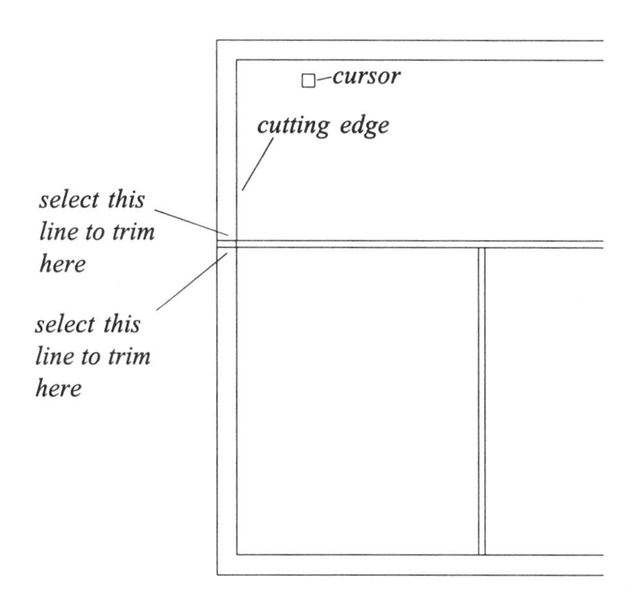

Figure 3.9. The new view using the Zoom command and the Trim command following it

- Turn **Snap** on.

- Select **Modify/Trim** and the comand line will prompt

Command: _trim	
Current settings: Projection=UCS Edge=Extend	
Select cutting edges ...	***select line as shown in Figure 3.9***
Select objects: 1 found	
Select objects:	***Enter***
Select object to trim or [Project/Edge/Undo]:	***select overlapping line***
Select object to trim or [Project/Edge/Undo]:	***select overlapping line***
Select object to trim or [Project/Edge/Undo]:	***Enter***

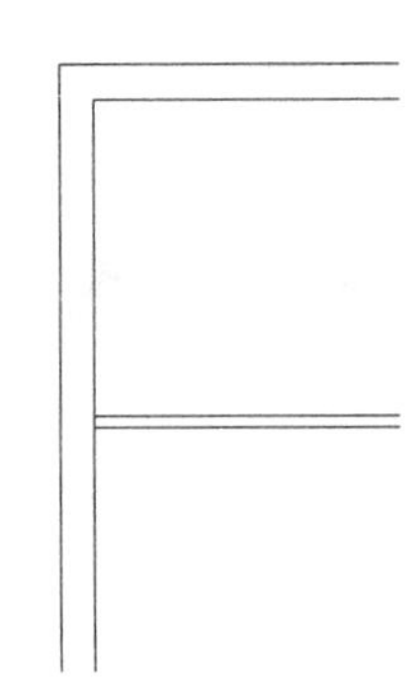

Figure 3.10. The completed Trim command

The modified drawing now looks the same as Figure 3.10.

We now need to use **Modify/Break** to erase the inner line of the outer wall where the newly trimmed partition lines touch it. For this we will use the **Break** command which splits a line into 2 portions, or forms a gap between 2 chosen points.

- Click the **Break** button from the **Modify** toolbar (you could also use pull-down menu **Modify/Break**) and the command line will prompt

  Command: _break Select object: ***(select line as shown in Figure 3.11)***

  Enter second point (or F for first point): ***f***

  Specify first break point: ***(select point as shown in Figure 3.11)***

  Specify second break point: ***(select point as shown in Figure 3.11)***

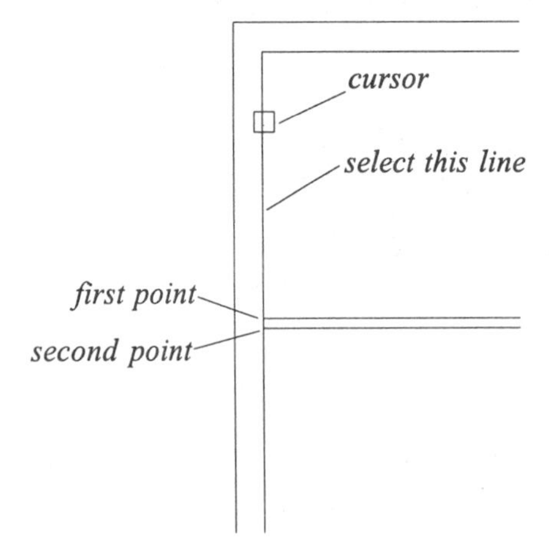

Figure 3.11. The Break command

Figure 3.12. The completed Break command

The completed **Break** is shown in Figure 3.12.

Closing Down a Toolbar

- From the menu pull-down menu select **View/Toolbars** and click off the **Zoom** toolbar that we loaded earlier or pick the **Close** button as shown in Figure 3.8.

Whenever we use **Zoom** from now on we will use the existing **Zoom** button from the Toolbar at the top of the screen.
Note that it is slightly different from the **Zoom** button which we loaded. It has an arrow in the bottom right hand corner which indicates that it is part of a 'flyout' i.e. clicking and holding the cursor on this will activate the remainder of the **Zoom** buttons as shown in Figure 3.13.

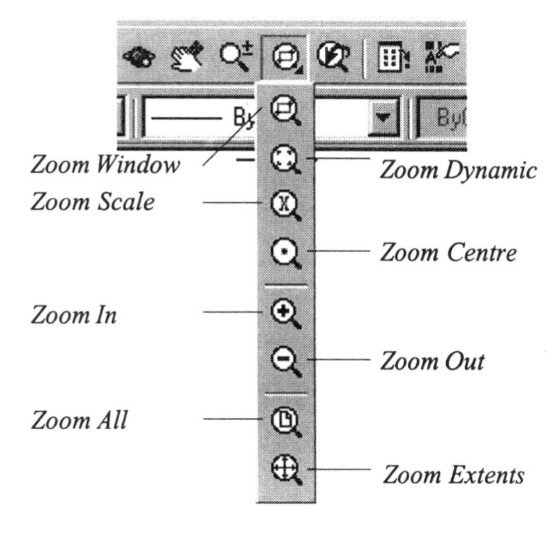

Figure 3.13. The Zoom flyout

Adding the Door Reveals

Remember that we set the **Grid** value to 1000 and the **Snap** value to 100 so your cursor will 'jump' every 100 units.

- Turn **Snap** on with **F9**.
- Turn **Grid** on with **F7**.

- Draw in the door reveals 1000mm wide as shown in Figure 3.14. Because **Grid** and **Snap** are on you will not need coordinates.

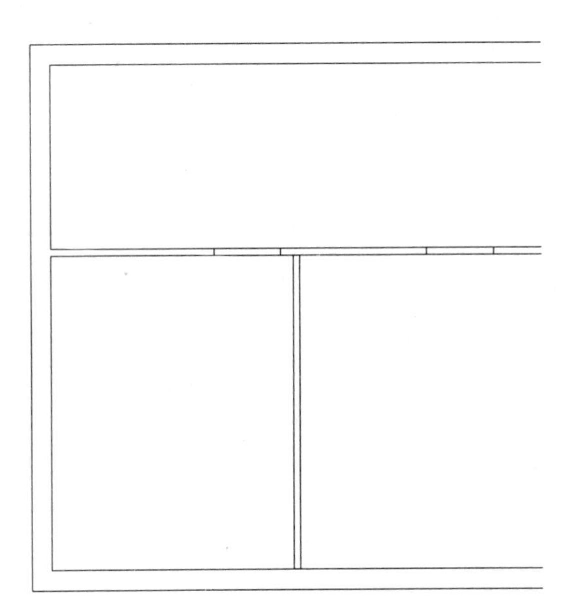

Figure 3.14*. The door reveals in the enlarged window*

Moving around the Drawing (The Pan Command)

- After you have drawn the door reveals in Figure 3.14 use **Pan Realtime** to move around the drawing and complete the remaining door reveals as in Figure 3.15. The positioning of the reveals is not critical so use your own judgement.

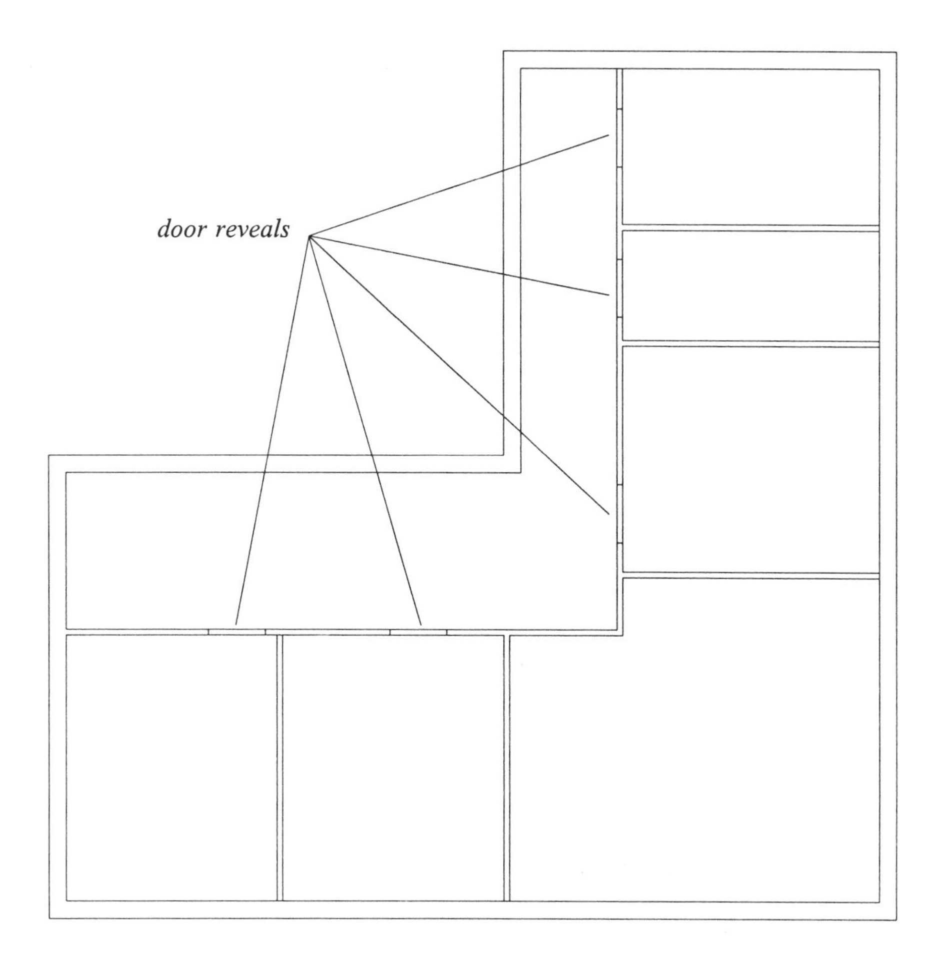

***Figure 3.15**. The completed door reveals*

Modifying the Drawing (The Break Command)

After completing the door reveals we now need to remove the lines between them to form the door openings as we did earlier in Figure 3.11 for the wall and partitions.

- Ensure that **Snap** is on.
- **Pan** to the area shown in Figure 3.16.

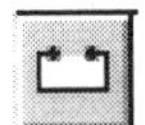

- Click the **Break** button from the **Modify** toolbar (you could also use pull-down menu **Modify/Break**) and the command line will prompt

  Command: _break Select object: ***(select line as shown in Figure 3.16)***

  Enter second point (or F for first point): ***f***

  Specify first break point: ***(select first point as shown in Figure 3.16)***

  Specify second break point: ***(select second point as shown in Figure 3.16)***

Snap is still on, so drag the cursor to the intersection of the door reveal and wall and pick that point as the **first point** and horizontally 1000 units across to the **second point** as shown in Figure 3.16.

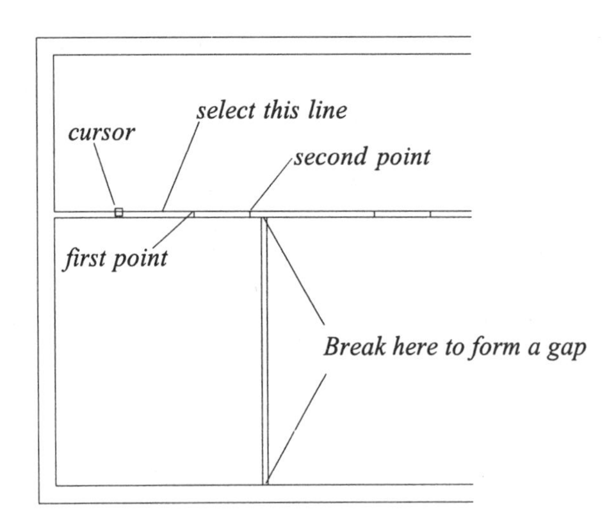

Figure 3.16. The Modify/Break command

- Repeat the process for the second opening on the same line and again for the line of the partition below it. Your drawing should now look like Figure 3.17. Complete the remainder of the doorways as shown in Figure 3.15.
- Use **Break** at the junctions of the walls to form a gap as shown in Figure 3.16.
- Again, **Pan** around the drawing to complete the partition, wall and door breaks.

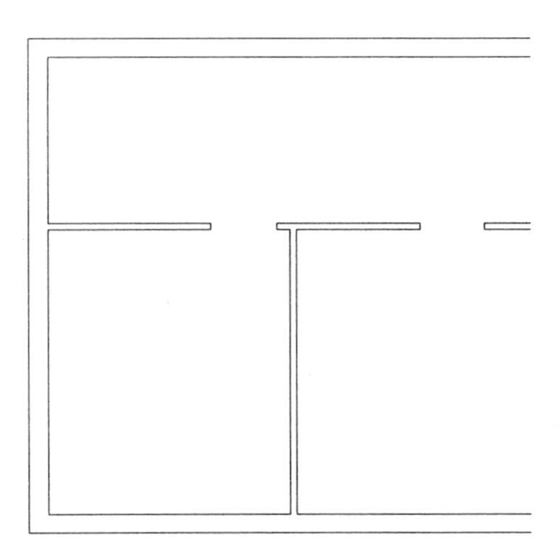

Figure 3.17. The completed doorways with the Break command

Modifying the Drawing (The Extend command)

To correctly form the double doorway to the Managing Director's office we must first extend one line to another to form the reveal as shown in Figure 3.18.

- From the **Modify** toolbar pick **Extend** and the command line will prompt

*Command: _**extend***	
Current settings: Projection=UCS Edge=Extend	
Select boundary edges ...	
Select objects: 1 found	***select first wall as shown in Figure 3.18***
Select objects: 1 found, 2 total	***select second wall as shown in Figure 3.18***
Select objects:	***Enter***
Select object to extend or [Project/Edge/Undo]:	***select first wall***
Select object to extend or [Project/Edge/Undo]:	***Enter***

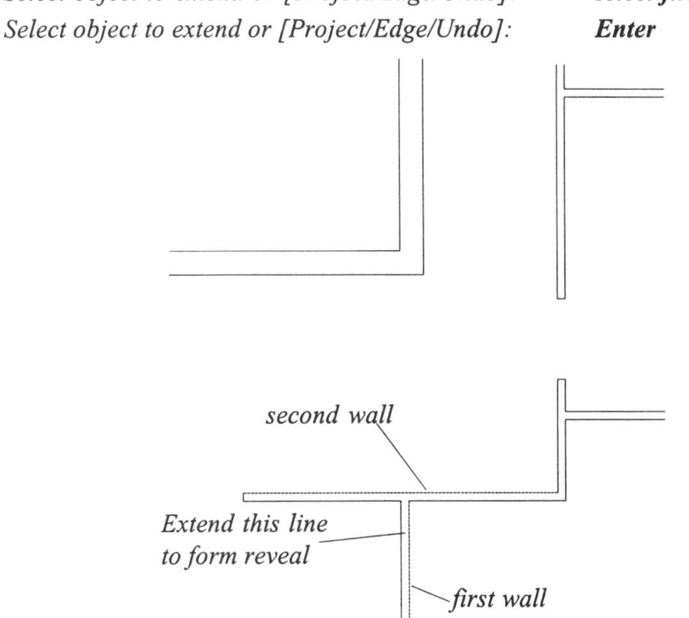

Figure 3.18. Using the Extend command to form the door reveal

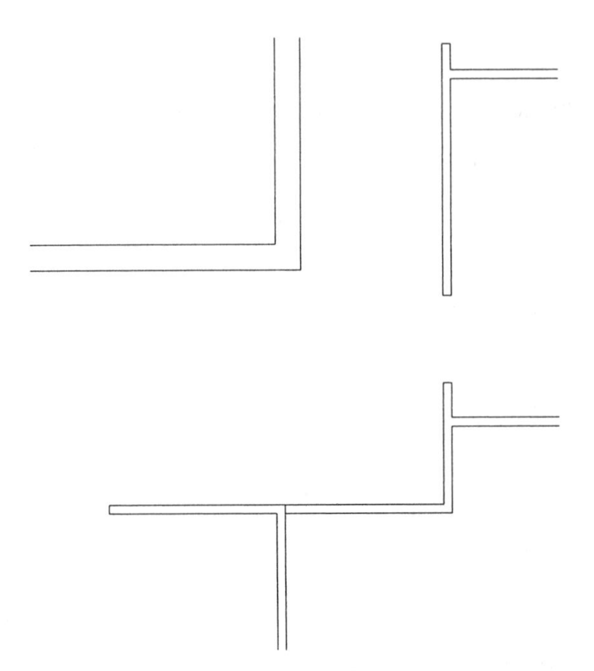

Figure 3.19. The completed Extend command

The walls will now look like Figure 3.19.

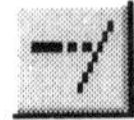

- We need to repeat the **Extend** command for the other side of the double door and the result will be as shown in Figure 3.20.

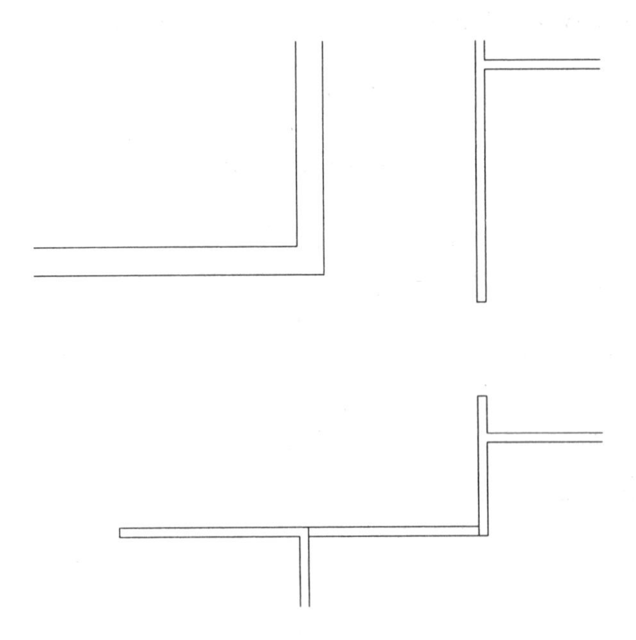

Figure 3.20. All lines extended

- Use **Modify/Break** to form the door opening to the Managing Director's office and complete it as shown in Figure 3.21.

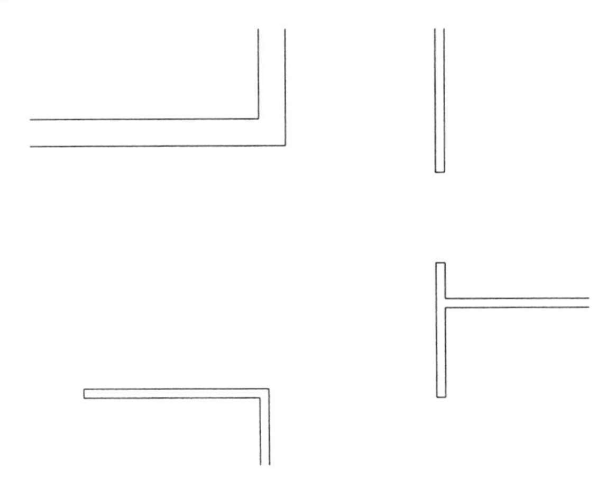

Figure 3.21. The completed doorway to the Managing Director's office

We now need to form the main doorway to the building.

- Use **Modify/Extend** to extend the external wall as shown in figure 3.22.

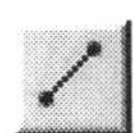

- **Draw** in the left hand door reveal and the window reveal as shown in Figure 3.22.

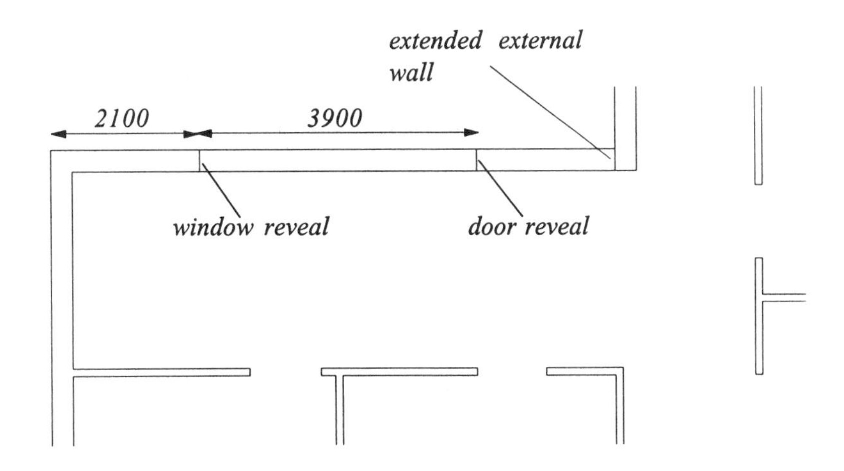

Figure 3.22. The main doorway and front window reveal

- Use **Modify/Break** to erase the lines in between the new door reveal and the extended line.

Figure 3.23 shows the new doorway.

Figure 3.24 shows the completed drawing so far.

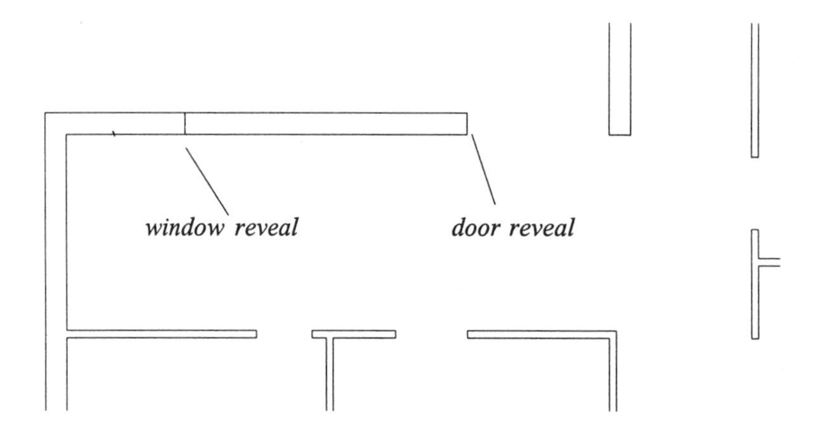

Figure 3.23. *The new front doorway after the Break command*

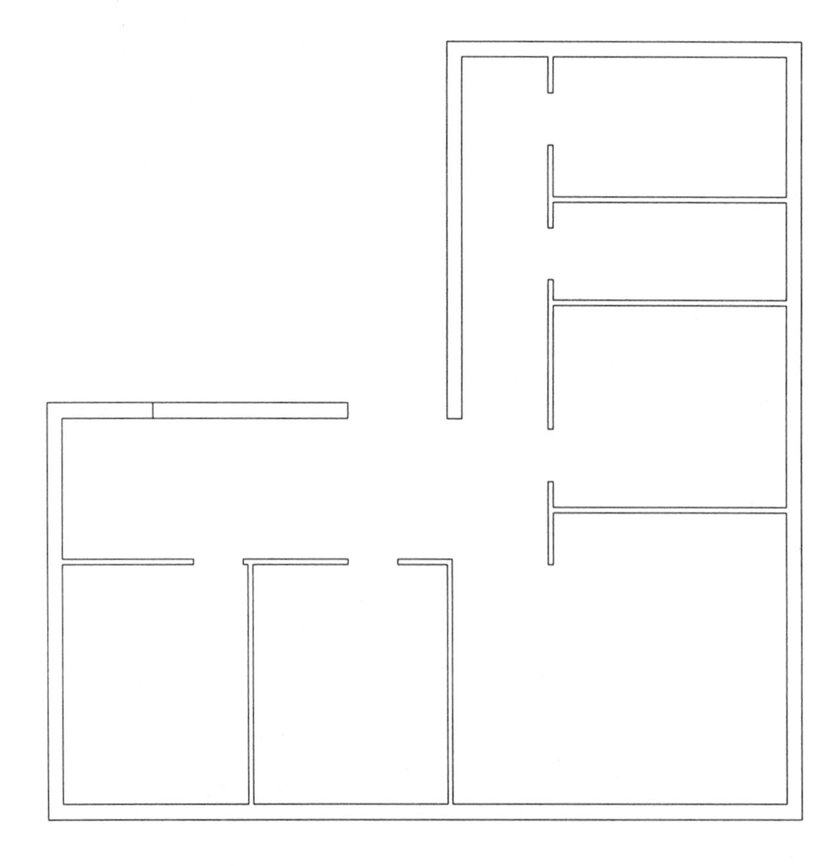

Figure 3.24. *The completed drawing so far.*

Chapter 4 — Drawing the Windows

Changing Layers

We have finished drawing the walls and before we place the windows we have to make the **Windows** layer the **Current** layer.

- Click on the **Layer** button in the **Object Properties** toolbar and the **Layer Properties Manager** dialogue box will appear as shown in Figure 4.1.
- Click on the layer named **Windows** and make it the drawing layer by clicking on **Current**.
- Click on **OK**.

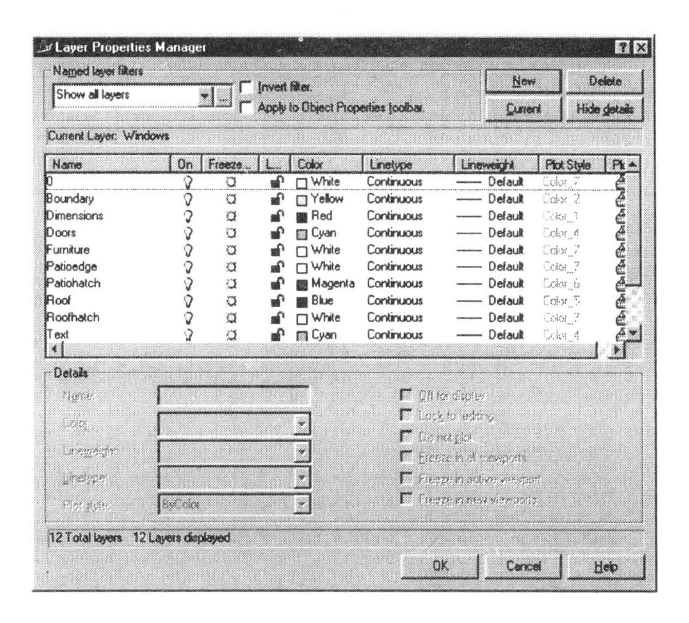

Figure 4.1. The Layer Property Manager dialogue box with the Windows layer Current

The **Object Properties** toolbar should now be similar to that shown in Figure 4.2 with the **Windows** layer **Current** and its **Colour** of **red**.

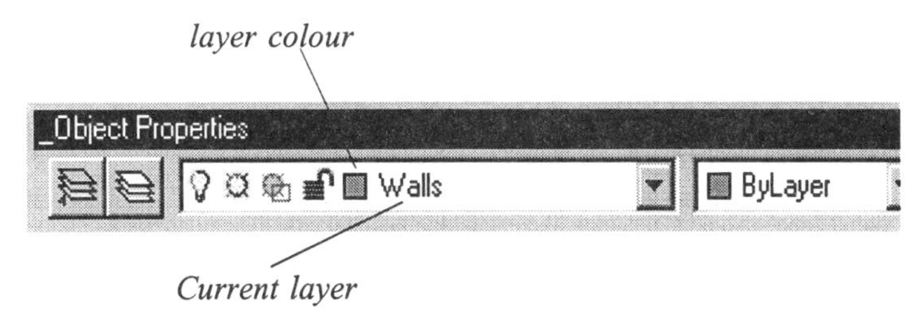

Figure 4.2. Object Properties Toolbar showing Current layer & Colour

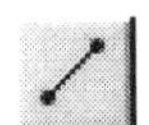

- Turn **Snap On**.
- Draw in the 100 mm wide mullion separating the window openings as shown in Figure 4.3.

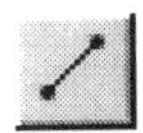

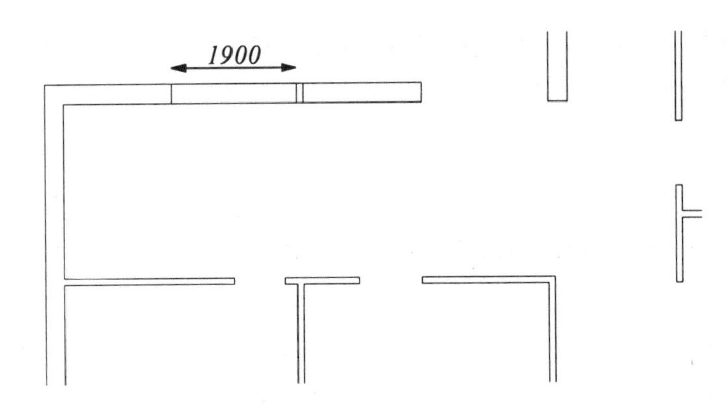

Figure 4.3. Window mullion in the front wall

- Draw in the 100mm wide window mullion at the building rear as shown in Figure 4.4.

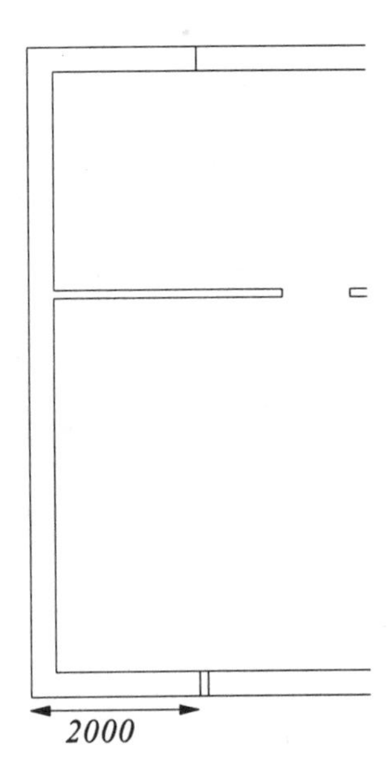

Figure 4.4. The first window mullion at the rear of the building

Copying Objects (The Array Command)

You can copy an object or selection set in polar or rectangular arrays. A **Polar** array, controls the number of copies of the object about a chosen point and whether the copies are rotated. A **Rectangular** array controls the number of rows and columns and the distance between them.

We are going to copy the side wall window mullion along the rear wall using the **Modify/Array** command. The distance between the mullions is 2000mm and we will use a **Rectangular** array.

- Pick the **Modify/Array** button and the command line will prompt

*Command: _**array***	
Select objects: 1 found	***(select mullion as shown in Figure 4.5)***
Select objects: 1 found	***(select mullion as shown in Figure 4.5)***
Enter the type of array [Rectangular/Polar] <R>:	***r***
Enter the number of rows (---) <1>:	***Enter***
Enter the number of columns (|||) <1>	*7*
Specify the distance between columns (|||):	***2000***

***Figure 4.5**. The completed window mullions using the Rectangular Array command*

■ You will now need to **Pan** across the drawing to the corner of the side wall so that we can draw the first 100mm mullion in the vertical direction as shown in Figure 4.6.

■ However, before drawing the mullion, use the **Modify/Extend** command to extend the rear walls as shown in Figure 4.6. Although the layer **Windows** is **Current** extending the walls will draw those lines on their own layer, **Walls**.

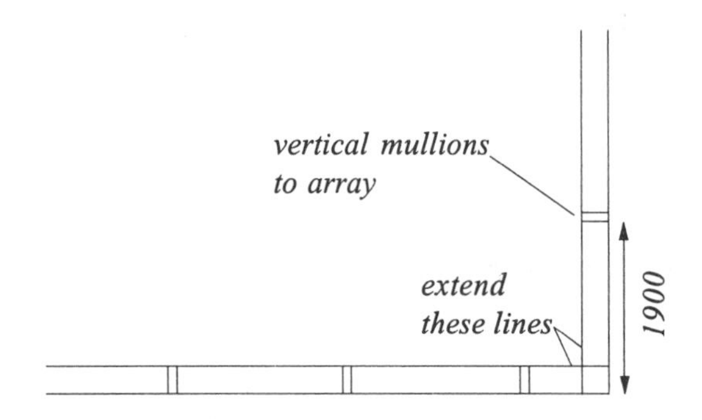

Figure 4.6. The extended walls and the first mullion on the rear wall

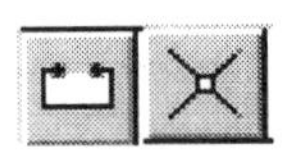

We need to **Break** the extended lines at the intersection of the inner wall and where they touch the outer walls as shown in Figure 4.7 to enable us to change the height of the walls later.
You will not see anything happening to the wall as the **Break** simply splits the wall at the **Intersections**.

■ Turn **Snap** on.

■ From the **Modify** toolbar pick **Break** and the command line will prompt

Command: _break Select object: ***(select line as shown in Figure 4.7)***

Enter second point (or F for first point): ***f***

Enter first point: ***(select point as shown in Figure 4.7)***

Enter second point: ***@ (breaks at the previous point chosen)***

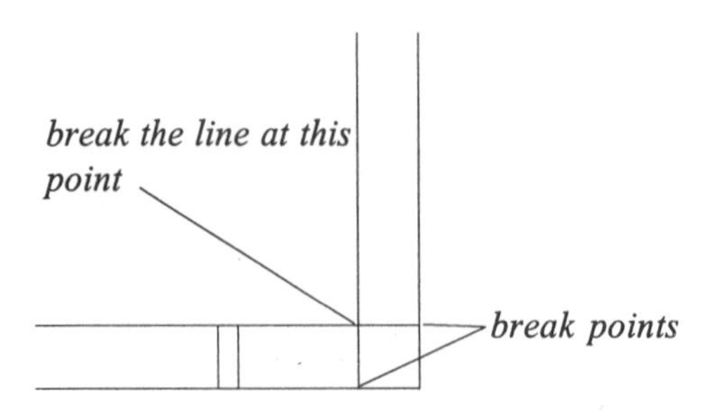

Figure 4.7. The Break command used to break at the points shown

- Repeat the **Break** command for the 2 outer wall lines with the break points as shown in Figure 4.7.

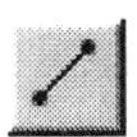

- Draw in the 100mm wide window mullion as shown in Figure 4.6, 1900mm from the building corner.

We will now **Modify/Array** the mullion but this time in a vertical row rather than a column. Figures 4.5 and 4.6 show the horizontal and vertical mullions which we have drawn up to this point.

- Pick the **Modify/Array** button and the command line will prompt

*Command: **_array***

Select objects: 1 found ***(select mullion as shown in Figure 4.8)***

Select objects: 1 found ***(select mullion as shown in Figure 4.8)***

Select objects: ***Enter***

Enter the type of array [Rectangular/Polar] <R>: ***r***

Enter the number of rows (---) <1>: ***7***

Enter the number of columns (|||) <7> ***1***

Distance between columns (|||): ***2000***

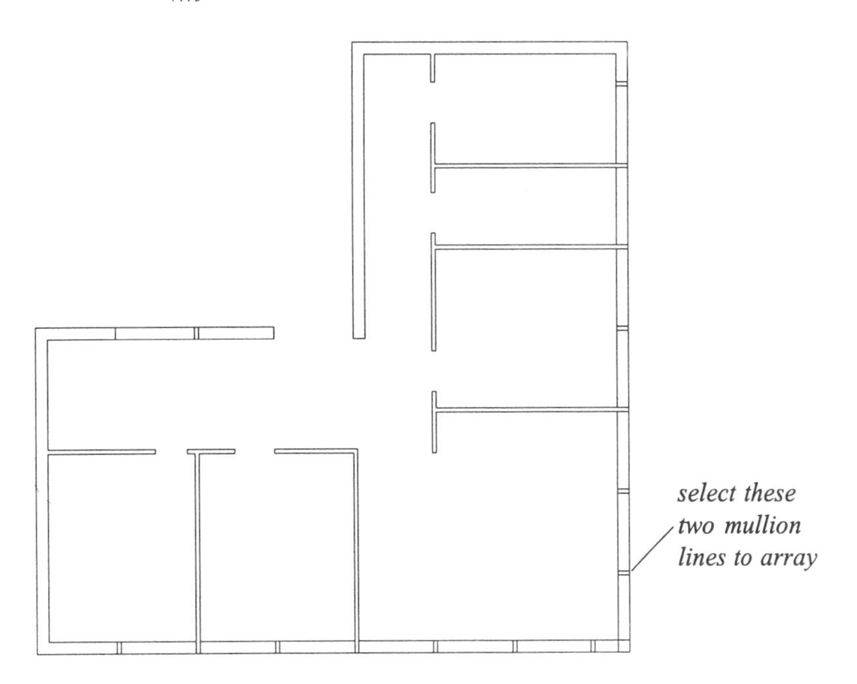

***Figure 4.8**. The window mullions after arraying vertically*

- Draw the 100mm mullion in the front wall as shown in Figure 4.9, 2000mm from the building corner.
- **Modify/Array** these 2 lines.

The difference this time is that we will array in a negative direction so the distance between columns will be preceded with a minus '-' sign.

- Pick the **Modify/Array** button and the command line will prompt

*Command: **_array***		
Select objects: 1 found	***(select mullion as shown in Figure 4.9)***	
Select objects: 1 found	***(select mullion as shown in Figure 4.9)***	
Select objects:	***Enter***	
Enter the type of array [Rectangular/Polar] <R>:	***r***	
Enter the number of rows (---) <1>:	***3***	
Enter the number of columns (|||) <1>:	***1***	
Specify the distance between columns (|||):	***-2000***	***(Don't forget the minus)***

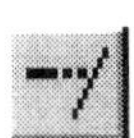

- **Modify/Extend** the inner wall line to meet the outer lines as shown in figure 4.9.

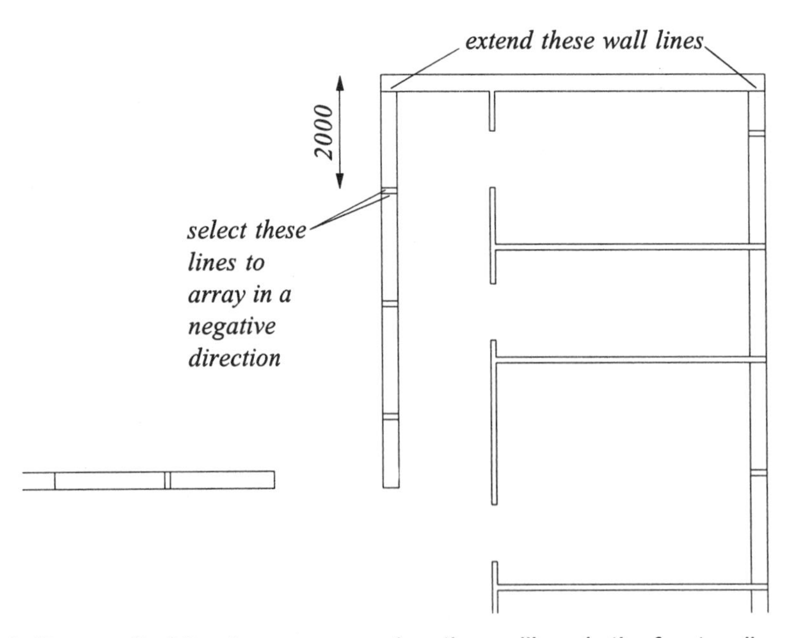

***Figure 4.9**. The result of the Array command on the mullions in the front wall*

Drawing with Object Snap

So far we have relied upon the **Snap** value of 100 and for **Snap** to be turned on for drawing to be carried out accurately. We can also snap to a location which may not coincide with the **Grid** or **Snap** setting. You can make an object snap, also called **Osnap** mode, permanent so that the cursor will always snap to an endpoint of an object, for example.
When using object snap modes you can specify a snap point at an **exact location** on an object. The mode determines the location. Running object snap modes can be turned on and off with the **Osnap** button on the status bar without losing your settings. You can use the **Tab** key to cycle through available snap settings. Object snap settings are stored with the drawing.

- Use **View/Toolbars** from the pull-down menu to load the **Object Snap** toolbar which appears as shown in Figure 4.10.
- Move it to a location on the screen suitable for you.

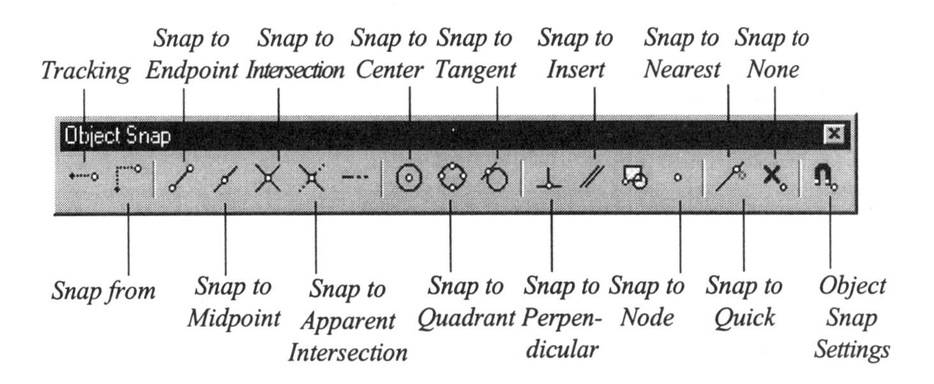

Figure 4.10*. The Object Snap toolbar*

Drawing the Glazing

We are now ready to draw the lines that represent the glazing.

■ Firstly, **Modify/Extend** the wall as shown in Figure 4.11 and completed in Figure 4.12.

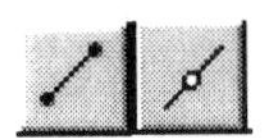

■ Draw a line from the **Midpoint** of the first mullion to the **Midpoint** of the second mullion as shown in Figure 4.11 and the command line will prompt

Command: _line From point:	***_mid of***	***(pick as shown in Figure 4.11)***
Specify next point:	***_mid of***	***(pick as shown in Figure 4.11)***
Specify next point:	***Enter***	

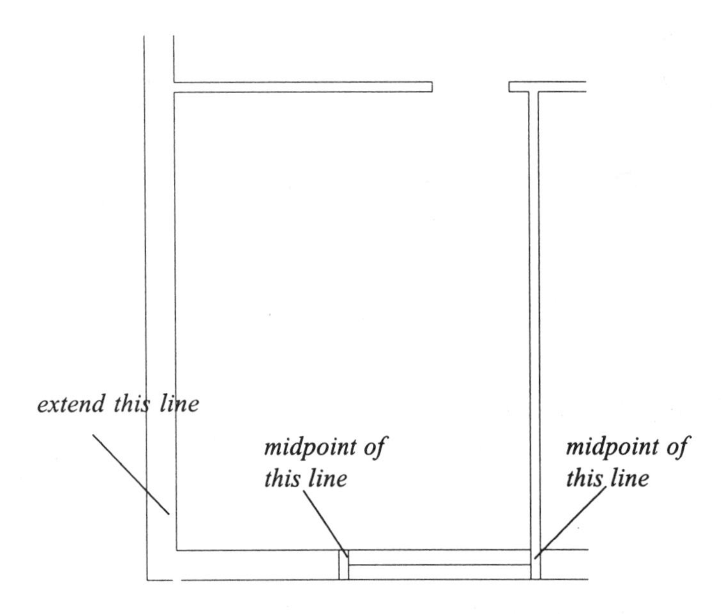

Figure 4.11. *Using Object Snap Midpoint mode to draw the glazing line*

Copying with the Offset Command

We will now copy the line by 20mm above and below it with the **Modify/Offset** command and then erase that line so the 2 new lines form the actual impression of the glass thickness as shown in Figure 4.12.

You may find that it is advisable to use **Zoom/Window** to enlarge the area.

- Use **Modify/Offset** and the command line will prompt

*Command: **_offset***

Specify offset distance or [Through] <1.000>: ***20***

Select object to offset or <exit>: ***(select glazing line as drawn in Figure 4.11)***

Specify point on side to offset: ***pick anywhere above the line***

Select object to offset or <exit>: ***(select the line again)***

Specify point on side to offset: ***pick anywhere below the line***

Select object to offset or <exit>: ***Enter***

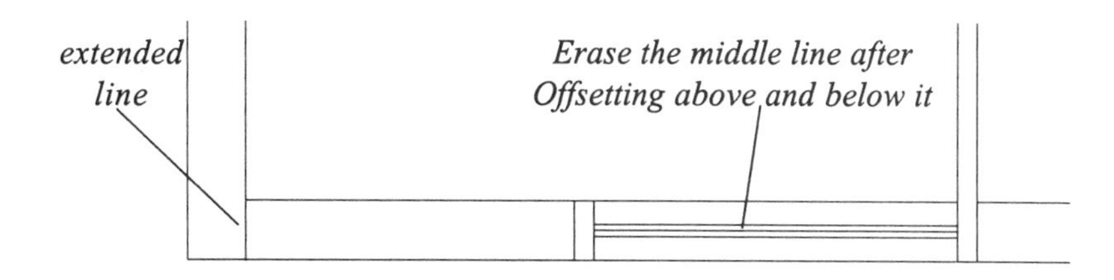

***Figure 4.12**. Offsetting and Erasing the middle line*

- Use **Modify/Erase** and select the middle line as shown in Figure 4.12 and the result is as shown in Figure 4.13.

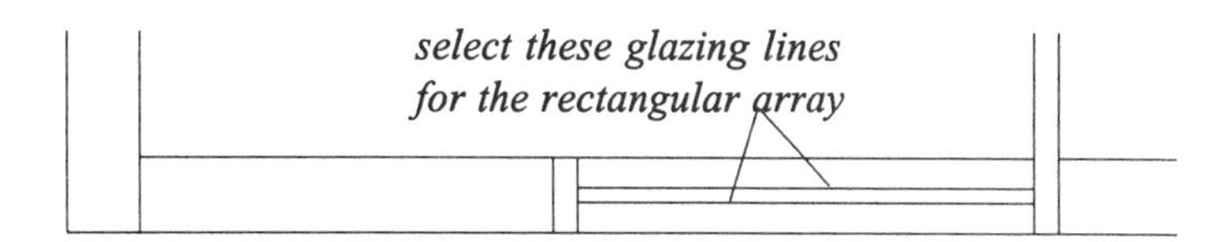

***Figure 4.13**. The result of Offsetting and Erasing the middle line*

We can now use the **Modify/Array** command to copy the glazing in between the mullions. The process is exactly the same as we used in Figure 4.3 but there are 6 columns instead of 7.

- Pick the **Modify/Array** button and the command line will prompt

*Command: _**array***	
Select objects: 1 found	***(select glazing line as shown in Figure 4.13)***
Select objects:	***(select glazing line as shown in Figure 4.13)***
Enter the type of array [Rectangular/Polar] <R>:	***r***
Enter the number of rows (---) <1>:	***1***
Enter the number of columns (|||) <1>	***6***
Specify the distance between columns (|||):	***2000***

You will probably need to use **Zoom/Out** to see the result of the array as shown in Figure 4.14.

- **Modify/Offset** the line upwards by 300mm as shown in Figure 4.14.

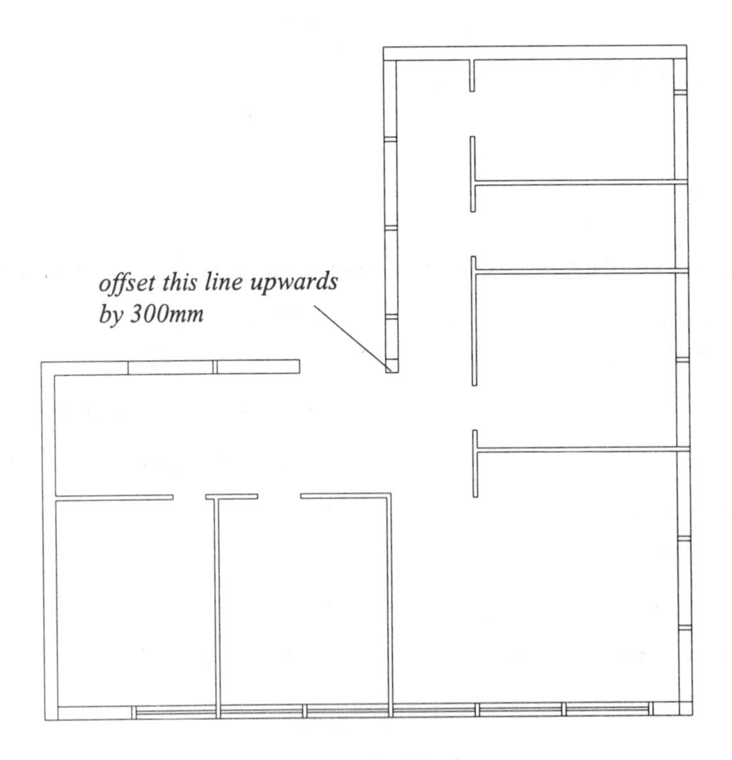

Figure 4.14. The result of the Array command on the glazing

- For the glazing along the rear wall, repeat the process by drawing a line in between the mullions as shown in Figure 4.15.

- Use **Modify/Offset** to produce the glazing lines as before.

- **Modify/Erase** the central line as shown in Figure 4.15.

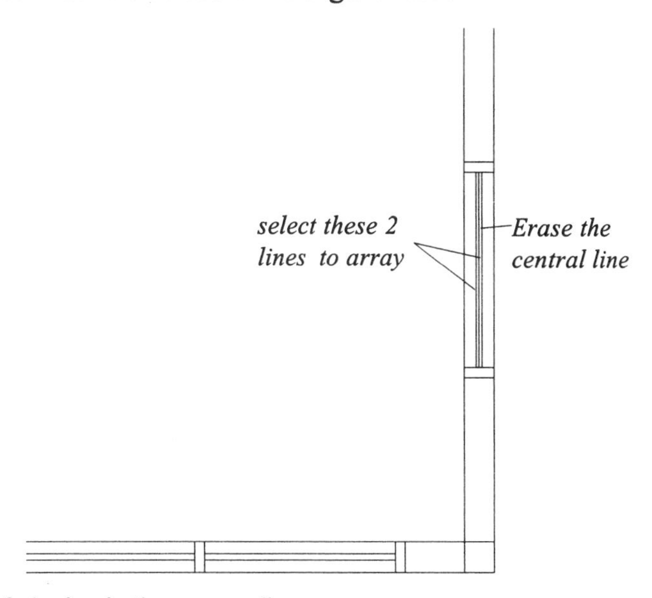

***Figure 4.15**. The first line of glazing in the rear wall*

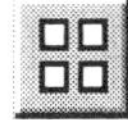

- Use **Modify/Array** to copy the glazing in between the mullions. The result is shown in Figure 4.16.
- Pick the **Modify/Array** button and the command line will prompt

*Command: **_array***	
Select objects: 1 found	***(select glazing line as shown in Figure 4.15)***
Select objects:	***(select glazing line as shown in Figure 4.15)***
Enter the type of array [Rectangular/Polar] <R>:	***r***
Enter the number of rows (---) <1>:	***6***
Enter the number of columns (|||) <1>	***1***
Specify the distance between columns (|||):	***2000***

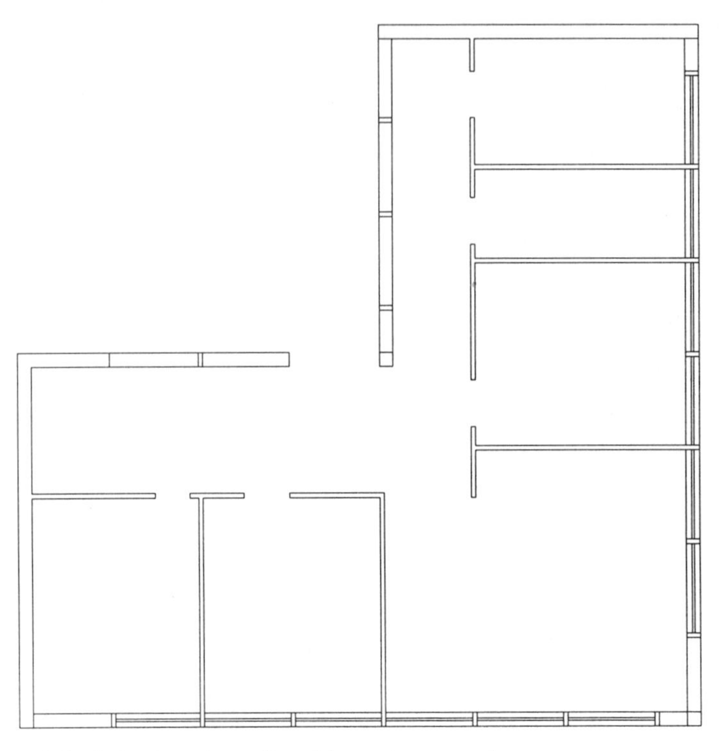

Figure 4.16. The completed glazing along the side and rear wall

- For the glazing at the front of the building you can use **Modify/Array** with 1 column and 2 rows, with 2000 between the rows. The 2000 will either have a positive or negative value depending on where you start. Can you remember why? If not, refer to the previous methods. The partly completed glazing for the front of the building is shown in Figure 4.17.

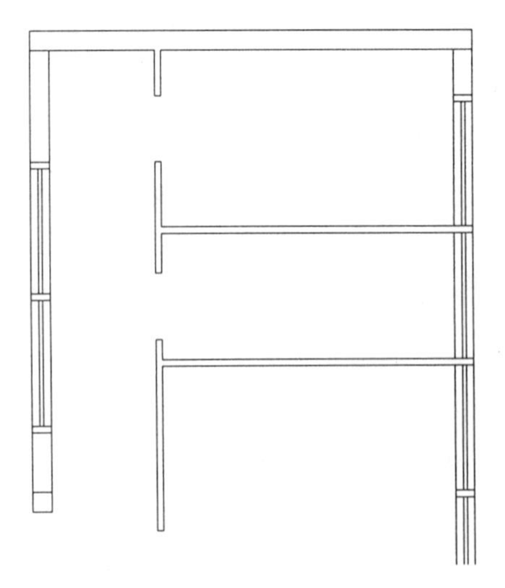

Figure 4.17. The partly completed glazing in the vertical front wall

- Use **Modify/Offset** to copy the main door reveal line to the left by 100mm to form the window mullion to the left of the door as shown in Figure 4.18.

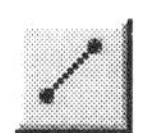

- Complete the glazing in the front wall as shown in Figure 4.18.

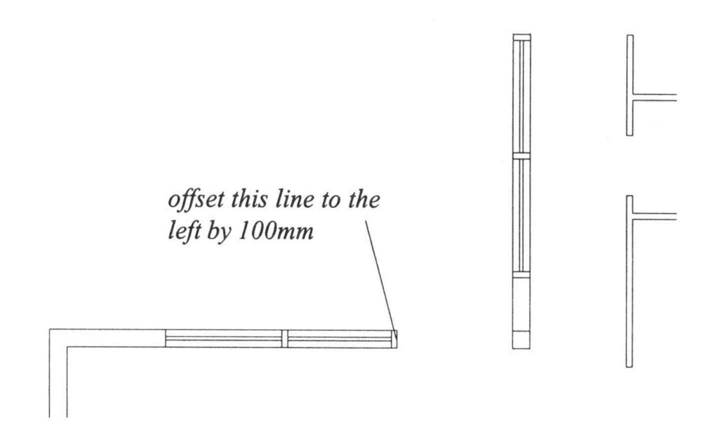

***Figure 4.18**. The partly completed glazing in the horizontal front wall.*

Figure 4.19 shows the almost completed glazing. We still have to draw the glazing in the building where it adjoins the corners as shown in Figure 4.19.

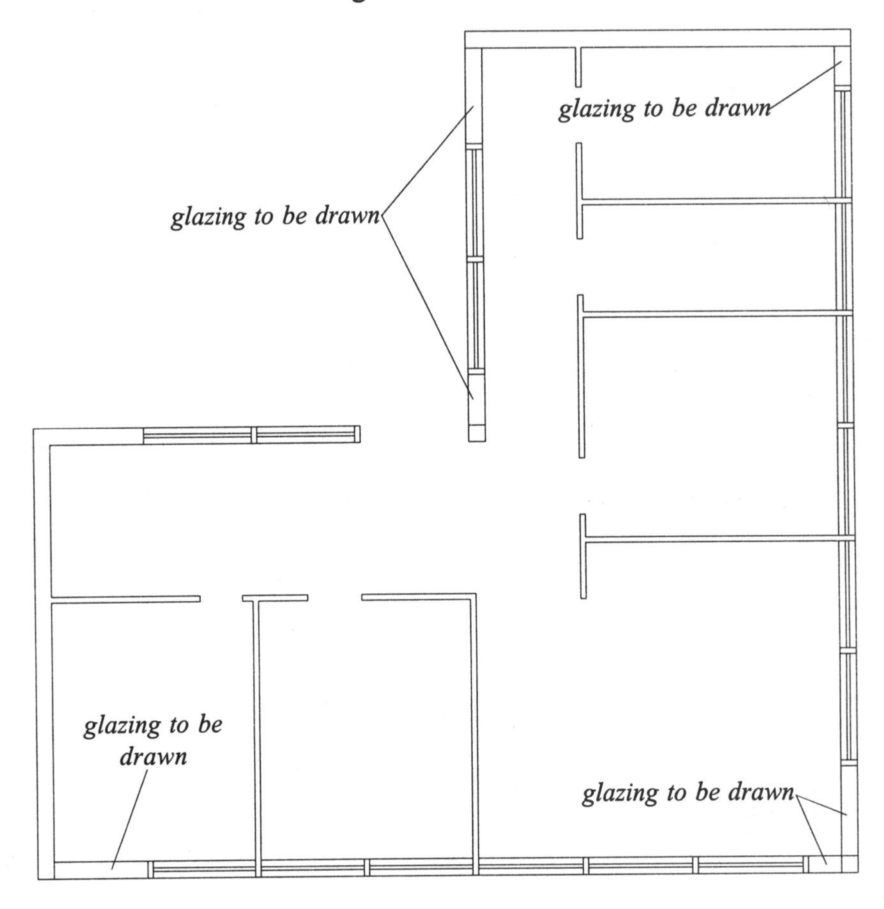

Figure 4.19. The building showing the remaining glazing to be drawn

- **Pan** to the area shown in Figure 4.20.

Using the same method as previously used we will draw a central line and **Offset** and then **Erase** the central line. This time we will introduce a different Osnap - **Perpendicular** as shown in Figure 4.20.

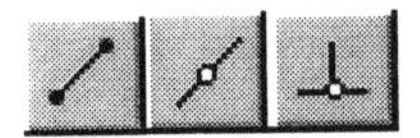

- Use **Draw/Line** and the command line will prompt

Command: _line From point:	***_mid of mullion as shown in Figure 4.20***
Specify next point:	***_per to inner wall as shown in Figure 4.20***
Specify next point:	***Enter***

Choose the **Midpoint** of the mullion line and **Perpendicular** to the inner wall line. Why do you think that we have used **Perpendicular** to the second line rather than using **Midpoint** again? Try **Midpoint** and you will see.

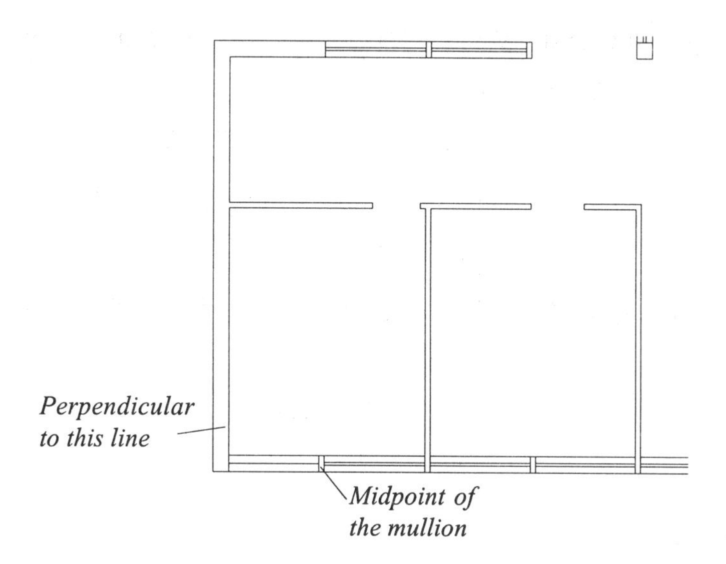

***Figure 4.20**. Drawing the odd sized windows*

- Offset the line by 20mm on each side.

- Erase the central line.

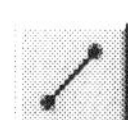

- Repeat this correctly for the remaining windows which adjoin a wall and the glazing is completed.

Next, we will complete the wall to the WC and draw in the doors throughout the building.

Chapter 5 — Drawing with Arcs

Before drawing the doors with arcs we will depict the double door to the WC as straight lines so that we can practice the **Mirror** command.

Copying with the Mirror Command

The **Mirror** command allows us to make a copy of an object about an axis. To mirror the 600mm long partition as shown in figure 5.1 we first need to draw an axis line.

- Make the **Walls** layer **Current**.
- Turn **Snap** on.
- Draw the 100mm wide partition 600mm long as shown in Figure 5.1.

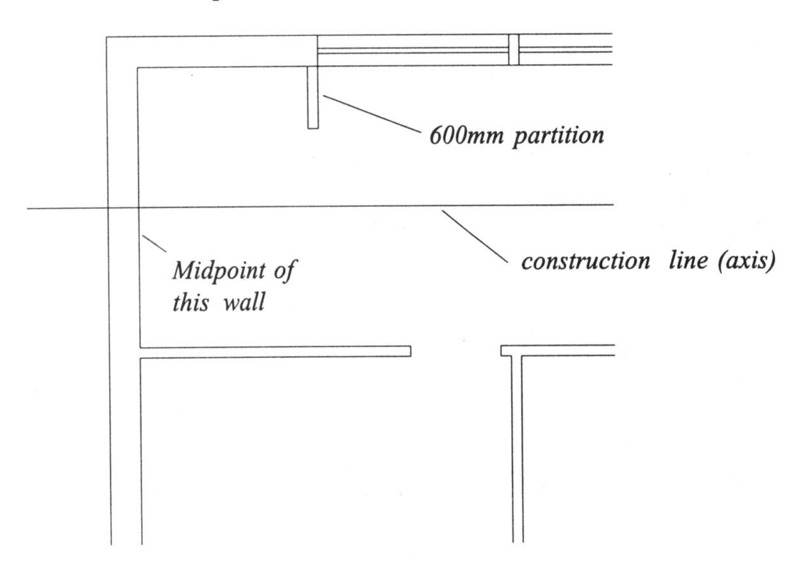

***Figure 5.1**. The construction line from the Midpoint of the wall and the drawn partition.*

- Turn **Ortho** on by clicking on the **Ortho** button as shown in Figure 5.2 which will allow only horizontal or vertical lines.

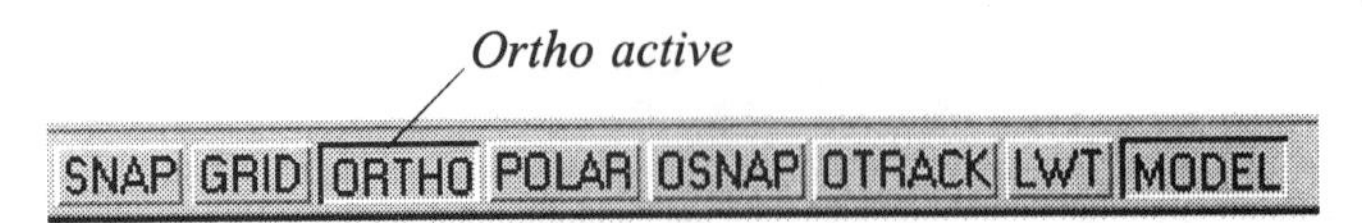

***Figure 5.2**. The Status bar*

We will draw a **Construction Line** from the **Midpoint** of the wall and in the direction as shown in Figure 5.1. This line is the axis in preparation for us to use the **Mirror** command and will be erased later. Remember that the line can only be drawn horizontally or vertically as **Ortho** is on.

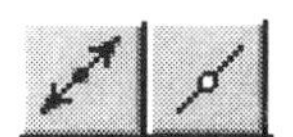

Use **Construction Line** and the command line will prompt

Command: _xline Hor/Ver/Ang/Bisect/Offset/<From point>:	***_mid of inner wall line as shown in Figure 5.1***
Specify through point:	***Draw the line horizontally***
Specify through point:	***Enter***

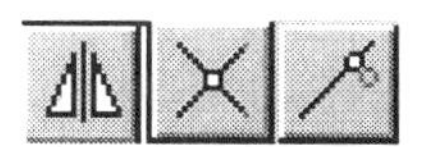

- Pick the **Modify/Mirror** button and the command line will prompt

*Command: **_mirror***	
Select objects: Specify opposite corner: 3 found	***(pick by window or individually as shown in Figure 5.3)***
Select objects:	***Enter***
Specify first point of mirror line: _	***int** of construction line and wall*
Specify second point of mirror	***(Nearest) pick anywhere on the construction line***
Delete source objects? [Yes/No] <N>:	***Enter***

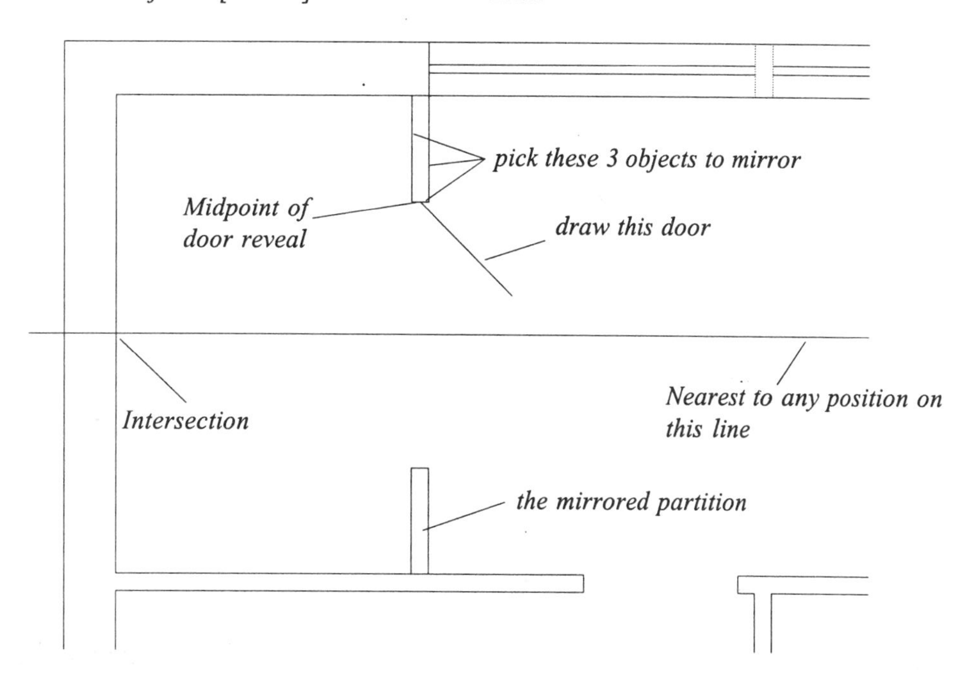

***Figure 5.3.** Using the Mirror command*

- Make **Doors** the **Current** layer.

- Use **Draw/Line** to draw in one of the doors from the **Midpoint** of the door reveal, 750mm long and at an angle of 315° as shown in Figure 5.3.

Command: _line From point: (pick the Midpoint of the door reveal)

Specify next point: ***@750<315*** ***(draws a line 750mm long at an angle of 315°)***

Specify next point: ***Enter***

■ Use **Modify/Mirror** again to mirror the door to the other side of the reveal as shown in Figure 5.4.

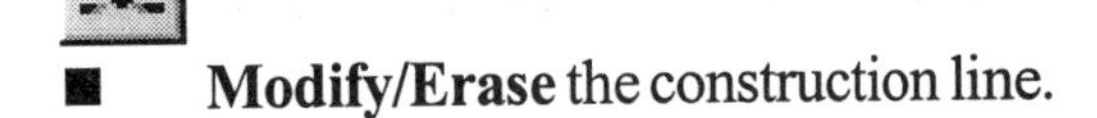

■ **Modify/Erase** the construction line.

■ **Modify/Break** the junctions between the new 600mm partitions and the previously drawn walls as shown in Figure 5.4.

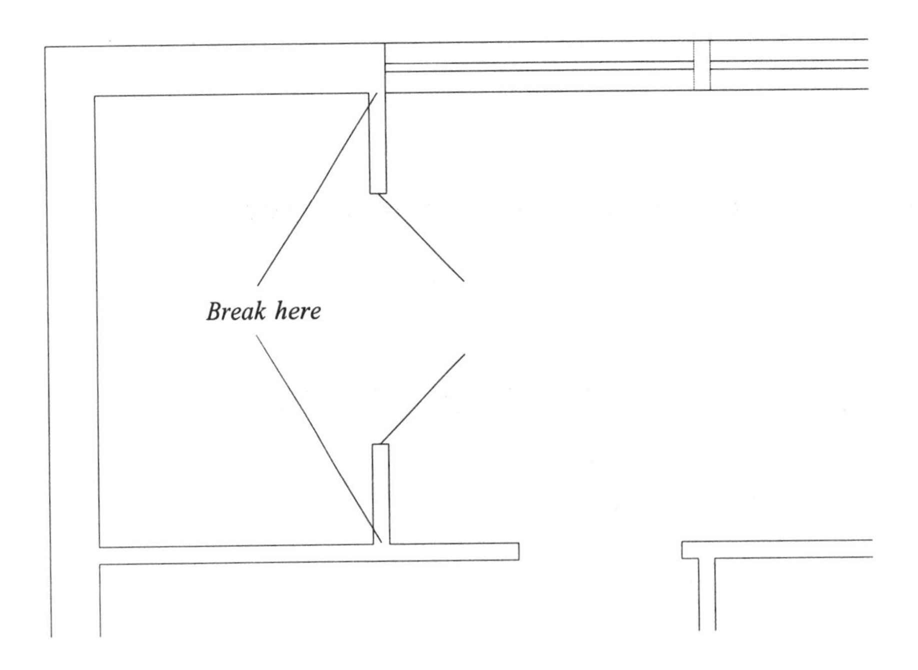

Figure 5.4*. Completing the 600mm partition and door lines*

Drawing Arcs

In AutoCAD, **Arcs** must always be drawn in an **anticlockwise direction** so the sequence of picking objects is crucial. We will use 2 different methods of drawing the arcs, the first by specifying the start point, the centre of the arc and the included angle. The second will differ by specifying the radius of the arc. We can draw in the arcs and lines to represent the doors but first, we need to change the **Current** layer to **Doors**.

- Make the **Doors** layer **Current** and ensure that the layer **Doors** is shown on the **Object Properties Toolbar**.
- From the **Draw/Arc** pull-down menu select **Start, Center, Angle** and the command line will prompt

Command: _arc Specify start point of arc or [CEnter]: _mid of **(select as shown in Fig. 5.5)**
Specify second point of arc or [CEnter/ENd]: _c
Specify center point of arc: _mid of **(select as shown in Fig. 5.5)**
Specify end point of arc or [Angle/chord Length]: *_a Specify included angle:* ***90***

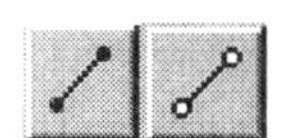

- **Draw** in the door line from the **Endpoint** of the reveal to the **Endpoint** of the **Arc** to complete the doorway as shown in Figure 5.5.

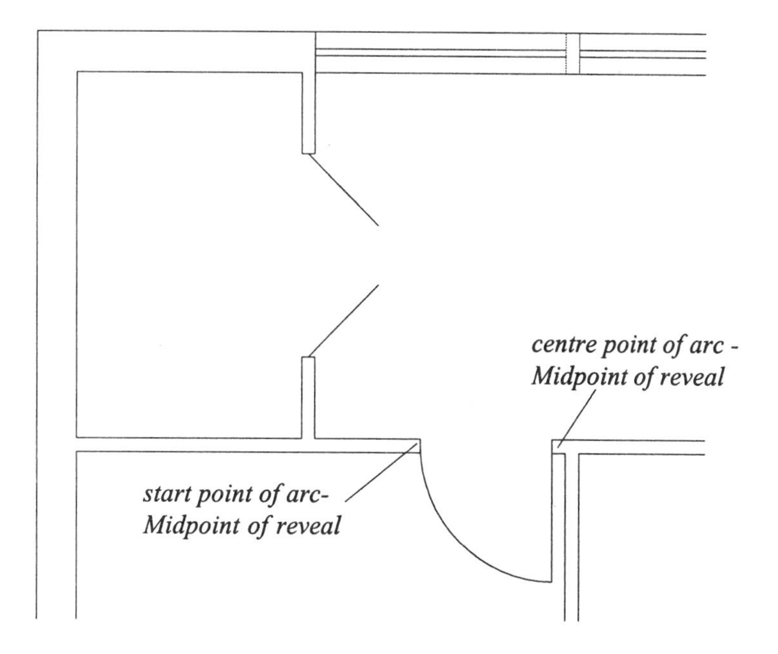

Figure 5.5 *Drawing the doors with arcs and lines*

As can be seen from Figure 5.6, the second doorway is scribed in the same way.

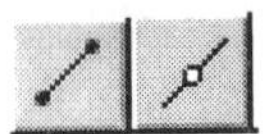

- **Draw** the door line from the **Midpoint** of the reveal 1000mm long as shown in Figure 5.6.
- From the **Draw/Arc** pull-down menu select **Start, End, Radius** and the command line will prompt

  Command: _arc Specify start point of arc or [CEnter]: *_mid of* ***(as shown in Figure 5.6)***

  Specify second point of arc or [CEnter/ENd]: *_e*

  Specify end point of arc: *_mid of* ***(as shown in Figure 5.6)***

  Specify center point of arc or [Angle/Direction/Radius]: _r Specify radius of arc: ***1000***

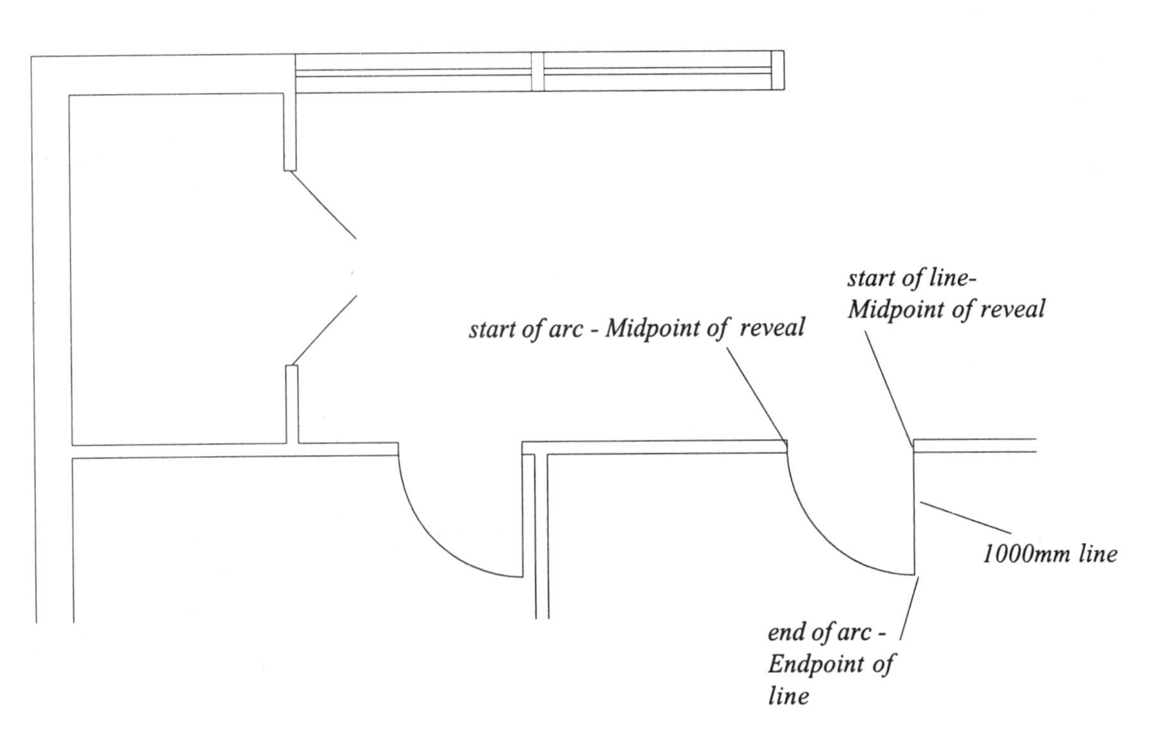

Figure 5.6*. Drawing the door swing with the Arc command*

- Complete the doors as shown in Figure 5.7 with the **Line** and **Arc** commands using either of the two methods shown above. All doors have a radius of 1000mm.

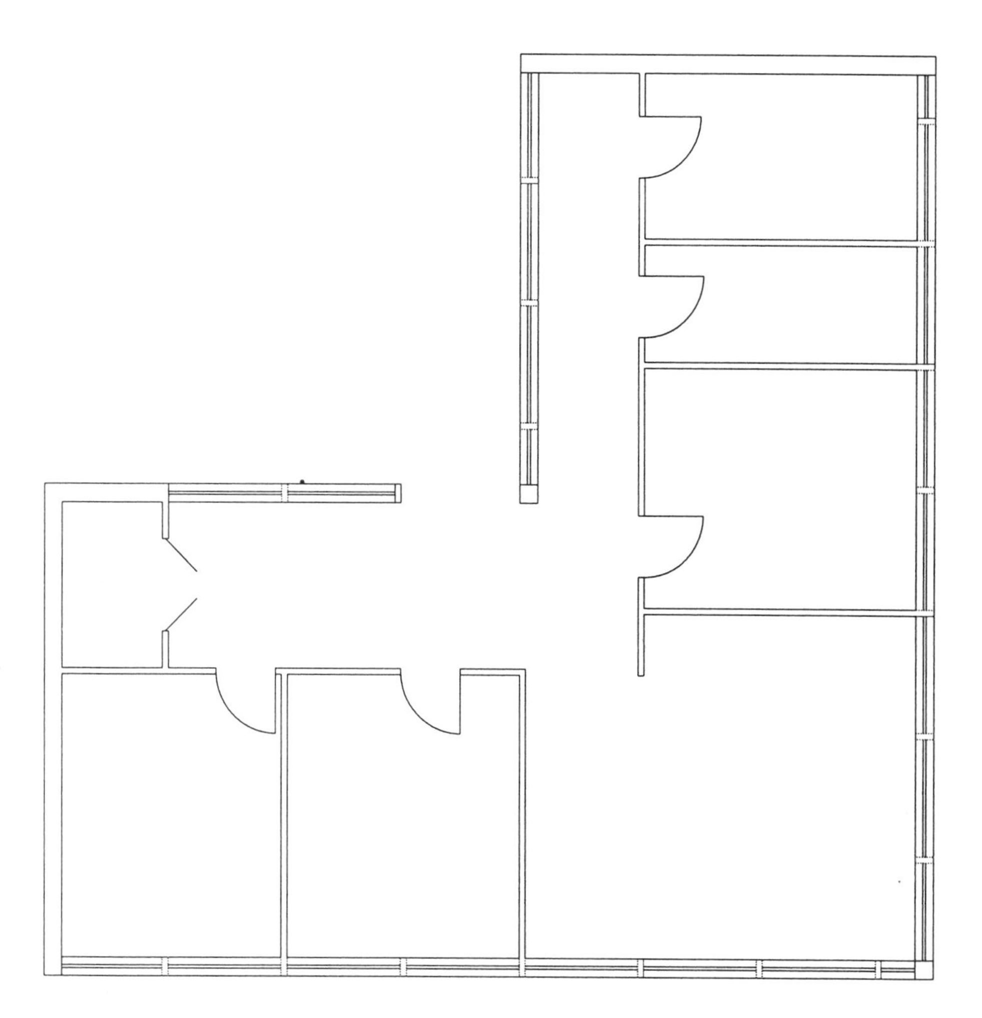

***Figure 5.7**. The completed doors*

To draw the front double door as shown in Figure 5.8 we will use the **Arc** command again but this time using the **Start, End, Direction** option.

■ Turn **Snap** on.

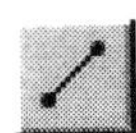

■ **Draw** both door lines 1000mm long as shown in Figure 5.8.

■ To draw the first arc use **Draw/Arc/Start, End, Direction** from the pull-down menu and the command line will prompt

Command: _arc Specify start point of arc or [CEnter]: ***(pick the endpoint as shown in Figure 5.8)***

Specify second point of arc or [CEnter/ENd]: *_e*

Specify end point of arc: ***(pick the point as shown in Figure 5.8)***

Specify center point of arc or [Angle/Direction/Radius]: _d Specify tangent direction for the start point of arc: ***(drag the cursor as shown in Figure 5.8)***

Because **Snap** is on, you can drag the cursor to the centre of the doorway for the **Endpoint** of the first arc and parallel to the **Start point** of the first arc to form the radius. The second arc is a repeat of the first but starting at the **Endpoint** of the first arc.

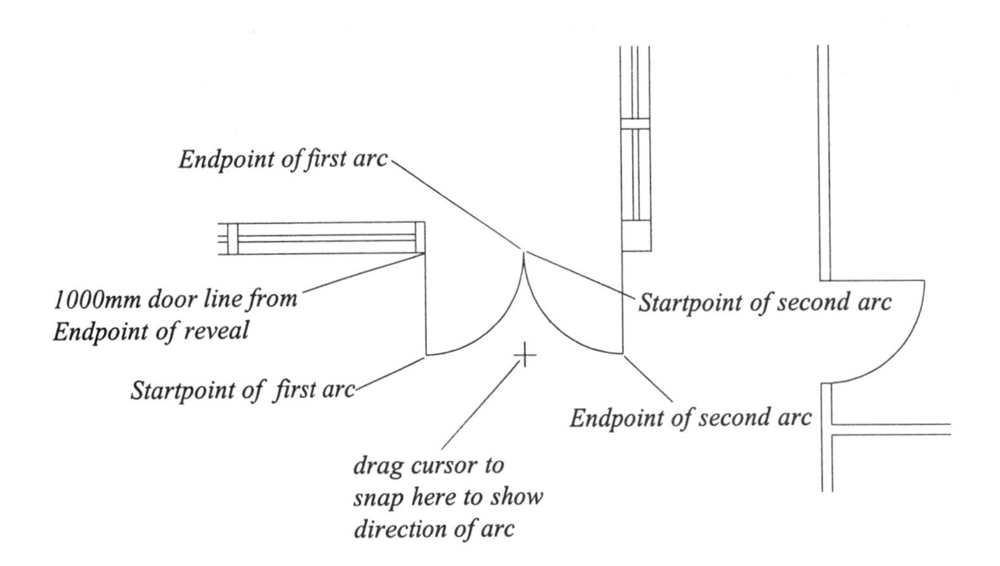

Figure 5.8. *Drawing the front double door with the Start, End, Direction option of Arc*

Chapter 6 — Making Repetitive Symbols

Re-usable symbols in AutoCAD are called **Blocks** and allow copies to be made of an object that is going to be used regularly. An added advantage of **Blocks** is that they can be resized during insertion into the drawing, making them larger, smaller, changing the ratio along the x and y axis or rotating to a different angle. A further bonus is that these symbols can also be used in other drawings, so symbols common to a number of drawings need only be drawn once. When a **Block** is made, AutoCAD assembles separate objects to form one object.

Rules for Drawing Blocks

Blocks drawn on **Layer 0** have a special adaptive quality. When a **Block** that consists of objects drawn on **Layer 0** is inserted to another layer, it assumes the color and linetype of that layer. The current layer's properties override any color or linetype assigned to that **Block**. If you draw a **Block** on any layer other than **Layer 0** it will retain the colour and linetype assigned to it.
A **Block** must also have an insertion point. This is a reference basepoint to which the **Block** is related and which you will use to position the **Block** when it is inserted into the drawing. When the **Block** is inserted into the drawing the cursor will be shown at the insertion point for that **Block**.

The Process of Creating a Block

- Make the **Current** layer **Layer 0**.

- Draw the objects which will compose the **Block** (which we will start from page 70).

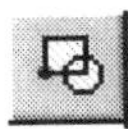

- From the **Draw** toolbar select **Block/Make** and the **Block Definition** dialogue box will appear as shown in Figure 6.1.
- Enter a **Block** name of up to 31 characters at the blinking cursor.
- Choose the **Block** insertion point with **Pick Point**.

The dialogue box will disappear and the command line will prompt for an insertion point. Use the usual methods of selection, object snap for example. The dialogue box will reappear.

- Choose the objects to be included in the **Block** defintion with the **Select Objects** button.

The dialogue box will disappear again.

- Select the objects to be made into the **Block** with the usual selection methods.

The dialogue box reappears.

- Click on **OK** and the **Block** is defined.

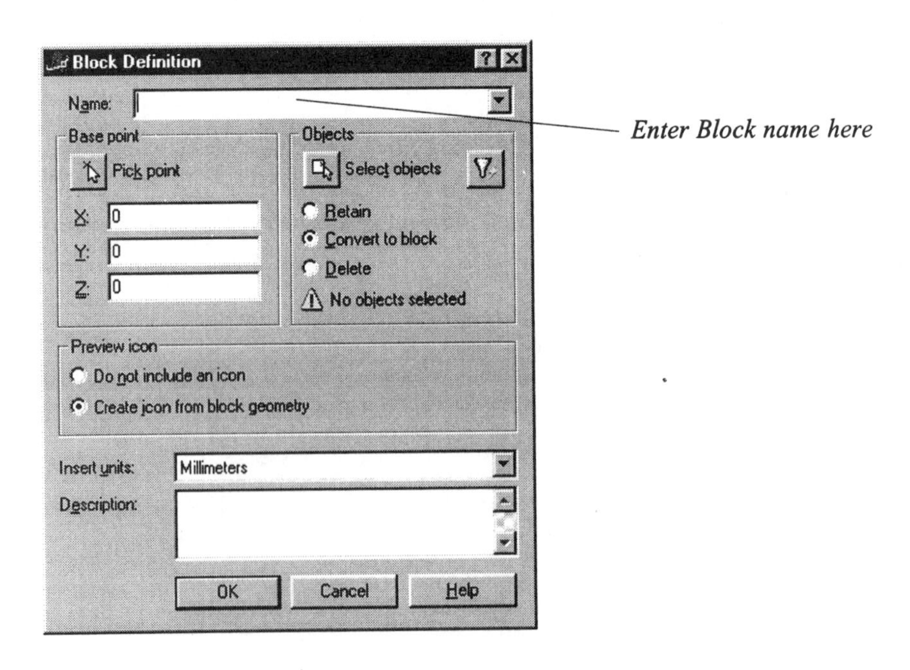

***Figure 6.1**. The Block Definition dialogue box*

The Process of Inserting a Block

- Make the destination layer for the **Block** the **Current** layer.

- Pick the **Block** button from the **Insert** pull-down menu and the **Insert** dialogue box will appear as shown in Figure 6.2.
- Click on the **Name** drop-down menu and a listing all of the available **Blocks** will appear.
- Pick a **Block** name as shown in Figure 6.2.
- Click on **OK**.

The command line then asks you for an insertion point, scaling factors and rotation angle if you have placed a check mark in each of the **'Specify on screen'** boxes. Ours show a check only in **'Insertion Point'**.

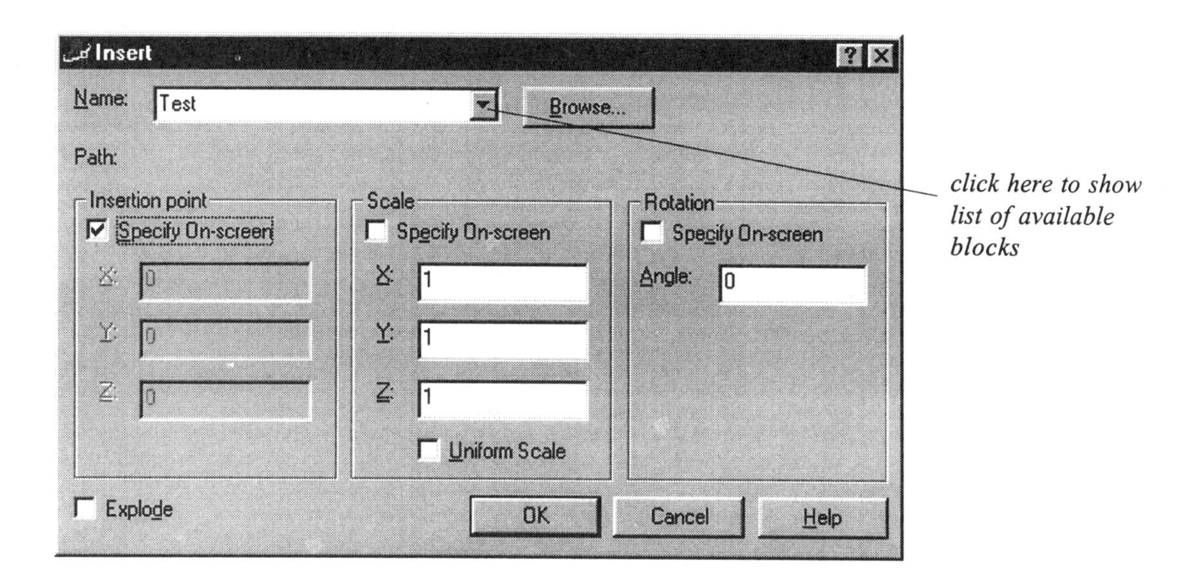

***Figure 6.2**. The Insert block dialogue box*

Creating Blocks for the Drawing

We will now create **Blocks** of the furniture symbols to be inserted in the drawing all of which are shown in Figure 6.16. We will practice new commands whilst creating each shape and then **create the Blocks after completing all of the drawings,** although in practice you can create **Blocks** at any time.

- Make layer **0** the **Current** layer.

- Ensure that **Grid** and **Snap** are on.

- Pan to a clear area of the drawing where the grid is in view and unobstructed.

The Filing Cabinet

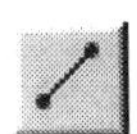

- **Draw** the Filing Cabinet to the dimensions shown in Figure 6.3.

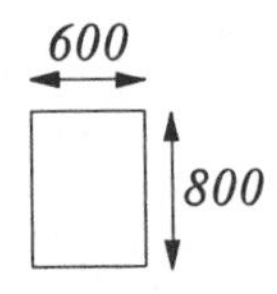

***Figure 6.3**. The Filing Cabinet Block*

The Low Table

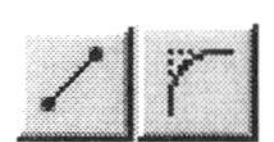

- **Draw** the Low Table to the dimensions shown in Figure 6.4.

- To create the rounded corners on the Low Table we must firstly set the **Radius** value.
- Pick the **Modify/Fillet** button and the command line will prompt

Command: ***_fillet***

Current settings: Mode = TRIM, Radius = 0.00

Select first object or [Polyline/Radius/Trim]: ***r*** ***(Enter r for radius)***

Specify fillet radius <0.00>: ***100***

- Re-activate the command by pressing the spacebar and the command line will prompt

Command: ***FILLET***

Current settings: Mode = TRIM, Radius = 100.00

Select first object or [Polyline/Radius/Trim]: ***Pick one line***

Select second object: ***Pick an adjoining line***

- Repeat this for the other 2 lines and the table should now have filletted corners as shown in Figure 6.4.

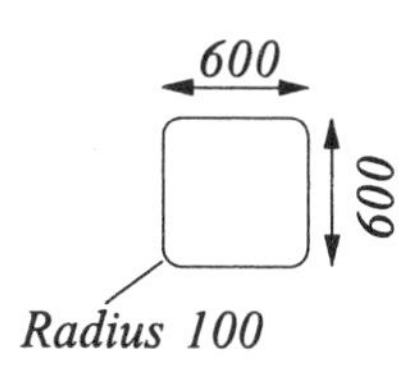

***Figure 6.4**. The Low Table with rounded corners using the Fillet command.*

The General Desk

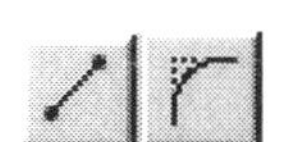

- **Draw** the General Desk using the same methods as you used for the Low Table and with the dimensions shown in Figure 6.5.

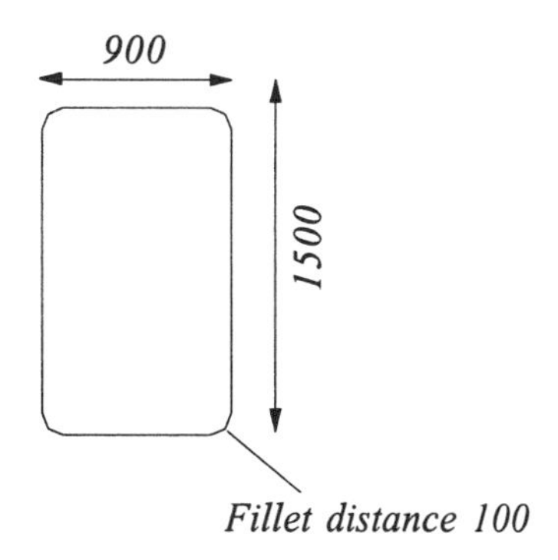

***Figure 6.5**. The General Desk with Filletted corners.*

The General Chair

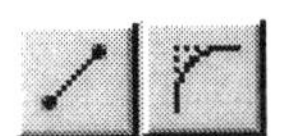

- **Draw** the General Chair using the same methods as you used for the Low Table with the dimensions shown as shown in Figure 6.6.

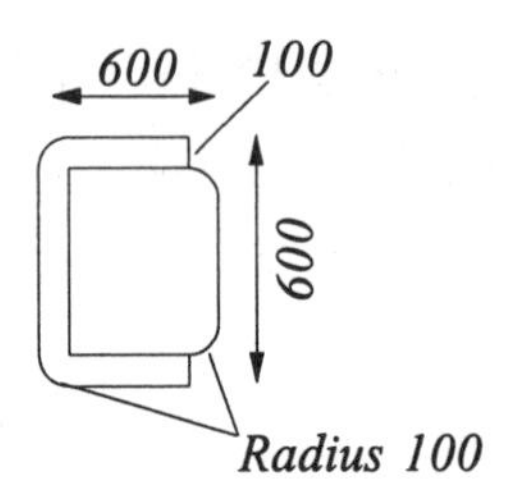

***Figure 6.6**. The General Chair with Filletted corners*

The Large Desk

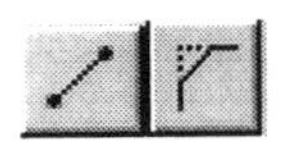

- **Draw** the Large Desk as a rectangle shape to the dimensions shown in figure 6.7.

To create the chamfered corners we must first set the chamfer distance values.

- Pick the **Modify/Chamfer** button and the command line will prompt

*Command: **_chamfer***

(TRIM mode) Current chamfer Dist1 = 0.0000, Dist2 = 0.0000

Select first line or [Polyline/Distance/Angle/Trim/Method]: ***d***

Specify first chamfer distance <0.0000>: ***100***

Specify second chamfer distance <100.0000>: ***Enter***

- Reactivate the command by pressing the spacebar and the command line will prompt

*Command: **CHAMFER***

(TRIM mode) Current chamfer Dist1 = 100.0000, Dist2 = 100.0000

Select first line or [Polyline/Distance/Angle/Trim/Method]: ***Pick a line***

Select second line: ***Pick an adjoining line***

Repeat this for the other 2 lines. The Large Desk should now have filletted corners as shown in Figure 6.7.

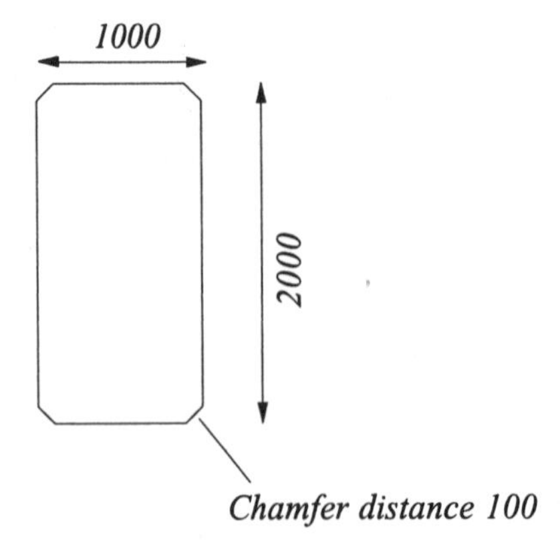

***Figure 6.7**. The Large Desk with Chamfered corners*

The Low Chair

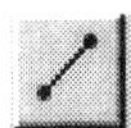

- Draw the 'seat' of the Low Chair to the dimensions as shown in Figure 6.8.

To draw the chair back with a thick line we need to use a line called a **Polyline**. A **Polyline** is a connected sequence of line or arc segments created as a single object to which can be added a line width.

- Pick **Draw/Polyline** and the command line will prompt

Command: ***_pline***

Specify start point: ***pick*** *the start point on the chair seat as shown in Figure 6.8*

Current line-width is 0.0000

Specify next point or [Arc/Close/Halfwidth/Length/Undo/Width]:	***w***
Specify starting width <0.0000>:	***100***
Specify ending width <100.0000>:	***Enter***
Specify next point or [Arc/Close/Halfwidth/Length/Undo/Width]:	***pick*** *rear seat corner*
Specify next point or [Arc/Close/Halfwidth/Length/Undo/Width]:	***pick*** *other rear seat corner*
Specify next point or [Arc/Close/Halfwidth/Length/Undo/Width]:	***pick*** *end of arm*

Remember that the **Polyline** is a single object even though it has more than one segment.

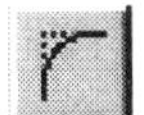

- **Modify/Fillet** the front corners of the chair seat and the rear **Polyline** corners and the Low Chair should be the same as shown in Figure 6.8.

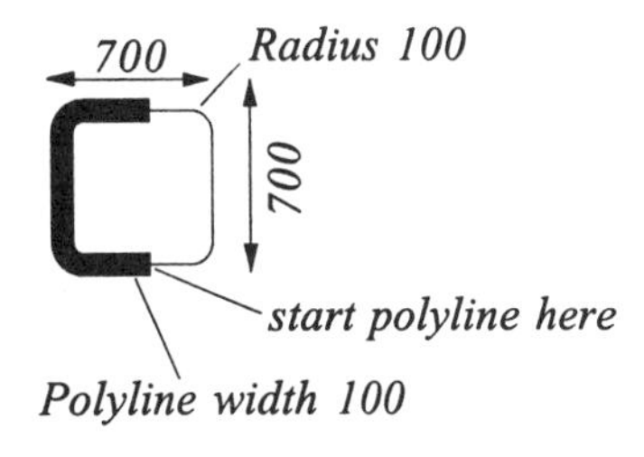

Figure 6.8*. The Low Chair with Polyline*

The Sofa

- The Sofa is created in the same way as the Low Chair and as shown in Figure 6.9.
- **Modify/Fillet** the lines before filletting the polyline.

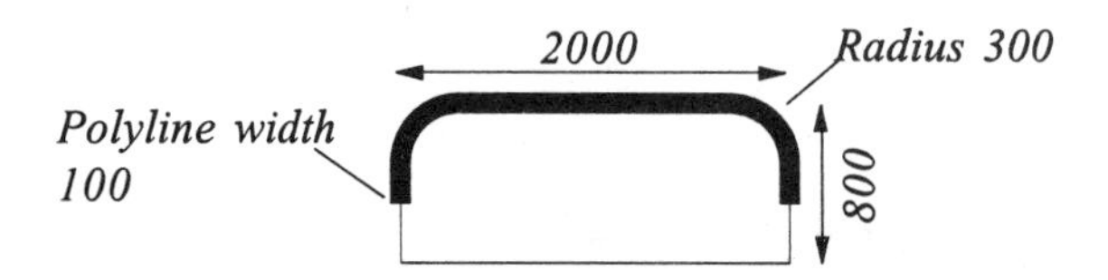

Figure 6.9*. The Sofa created with Lines, Polyline and Filletting*

The Director Desk

- The construction of the Director Desk follows the same process as the Low Chair and Sofa but the **Fillet/Radius** value is 300mm as shown in Figure 6.10.
- **Modify/Fillet** the lines before filletting the polyline.

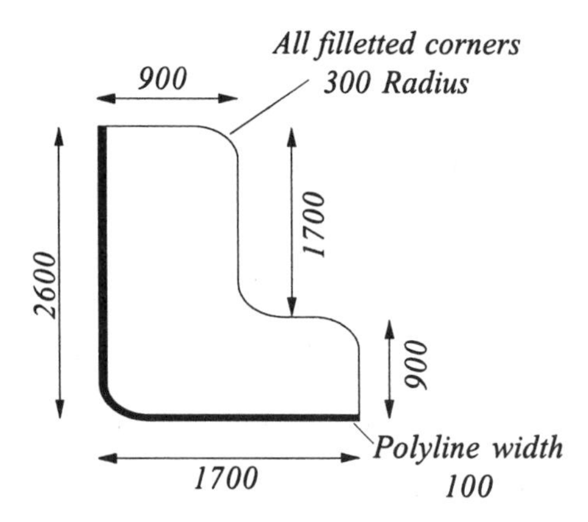

Figure 6.10*. The Director Desk*

The Operators' Chair

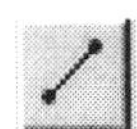

- Draw the square outline of the Operators' Chair to the dimensions shown in Figure 6.11.

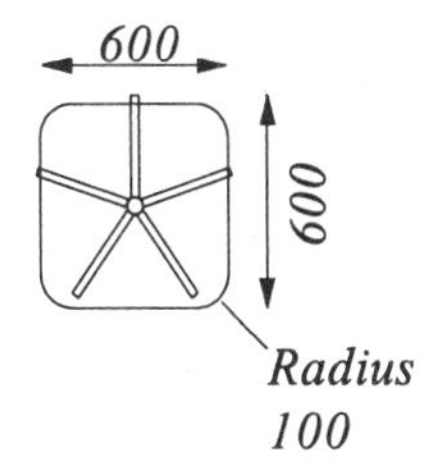

Figure 6.11. The completed Operators' Chair

To construct the chair plinth we will use the **Modify/Polar Array** option to copy the legs around the central chair stem depicted here with a circle set in the centre of the square.

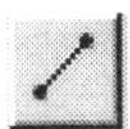

- Draw 2 diagonal lines as shown in Figure 6.12.

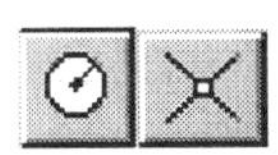

- Draw a 25mm radius circle at the **Intersection** of the 2 construction lines as shown in Figure 6.12.
- Use **Draw/Circle** command and the command line will prompt

Command: _circle Specify center point for circle or [3P/2P/Ttr (tan tan radius)]: ***int*** *of the diagonals*

Specify radius of circle or [Diameter]: ***25*** *Enter*

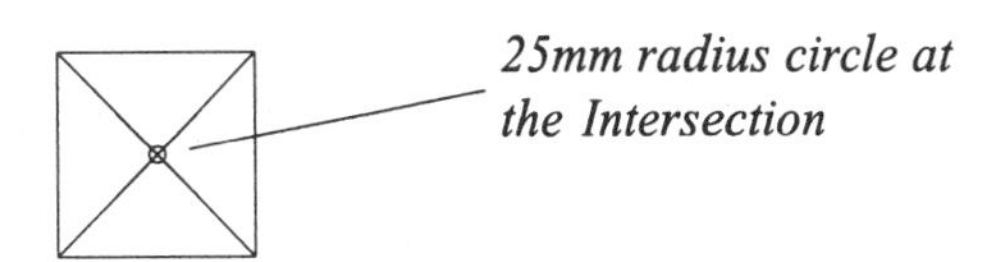

Figure 6.12. The 2 diagonal construction lines and the circle

- Erase the construction lines.
- Turn **Snap** off.

We will now draw the plinth by using the **Polyline** command to draw one leg placed at the 12 o'clock **Quadrant** of the 25mm circle as shown in Figure 6.13.

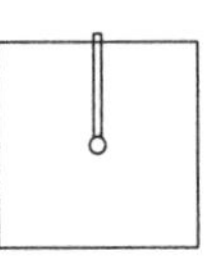

Figure 6.13. *The Chair leg drawn with a Polyline at the Quadrant of the Circle.*

- You will probably need to **Zoom/Window** to the area just larger than the Chair.

- Pick **Draw/Polyline** and the command line will prompt

Command: _pline	
From point:	***_qua of (pick** the 12 o'clock position on the circle)*
Current line-width is 100.00	
Specify next point or [Arc/Close/Halfwidth/Length/Undo/Width]:	***w***
Starting width <0.0000>:	***0***
Ending width <0.0000>:	***Enter***
Specify next point or [Arc/Close/Halfwidth/Length/Undo/Width]:	***@12.5<180***
Specify next point or [Arc/Close/Halfwidth/Length/Undo/Width]:	***@300<90***
Specify next point or [Arc/Close/Halfwidth/Length/Undo/Width]:	***@25<0***
Specify next point or [Arc/Close/Halfwidth/Length/Undo/Width]:	***@300<270***
Specify next point or [Arc/Close/Halfwidth/Length/Undo/Width]:	***c** (for Close)*

We can now copy the chair leg with the **Modify/Array/Polar** command to place 5 legs around the central shaft with the **Centre** of the **Polar** array being the **Centre** of the circle as shown in Figure 6.12. Why did we draw the chair leg with a **Polyline**? To make it easier to pick when we **Array** it - remember that **Polylines** are 1 object so with 1 pick all of the chair leg segments can be chosen.

- Pick **Modify/Array** and the command line will prompt

  Command: _array

  Select objects: 1 found — ***pick the chair leg***

  Select objects: — ***Enter***

  Enter the type of array [Rectangular/Polar] <R>: — ***p***

  Specify center point of array: _cen of — ***pick the perimeter of the circle***

  Enter the number of items in the array: — ***5***

  Specify the angle to fill (+=ccw, -=cw) <360>: — ***Enter***

  Rotate arrayed objects? [Yes/No] <Y>: — ***Enter***

- **Modify/Fillet** the corners of the chair with a 100mm radius.

The WC

- Turn **Snap** on.
- **Draw** the WC to the dimensions shown in Figure 6.14.
- **Modify/Fillet** the corners.

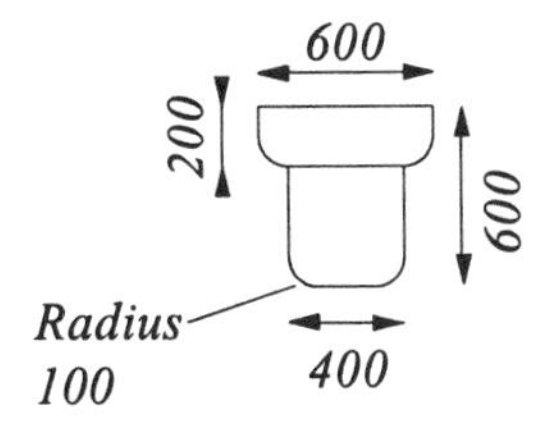

***Figure 6.14**. The WC with Filletted corners*

The Wash Hand Basin

- **Draw** the outline of the Wash Hand Basin to the dimensions shown in Figure 6.15.
- Turn **Ortho On**.
- Pick the **Draw/Ellipse** command for the basin shape and the command line will prompt

*Command: **_ellipse***

Specify axis endpoint of ellipse or [Arc/Center]:	***pick** 1st point as shown in Figure 6.14*
Specify other endpoint of axis:	***pick** 2nd point as shown in Figure 6.14*
Specify distance to other axis or [Rotation]:	***pick** 3rd point as shown in Figure 6.14*

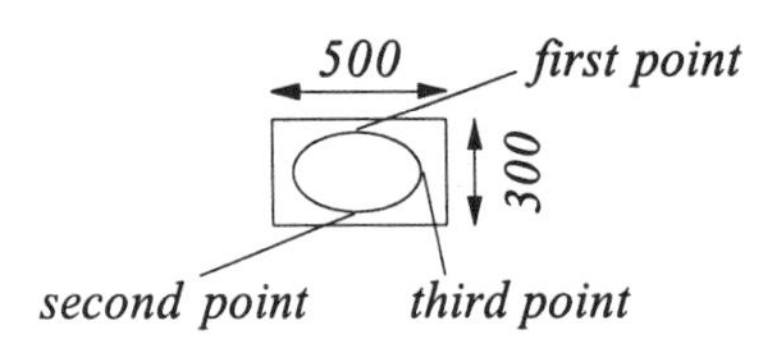

***Figure 6.15**. The Wash Hand Basin drawn with the Ellipse command*

The Planter

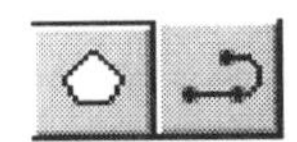

- Turn **Ortho Off**.
- To draw the Planter we will first use the **Polygon** command to draw an **Inscribed** polygon (i.e. where the points of the sides would touch an imaginary circle drawn outside the polygon).
- We will then draw the plant with a freedrawn **Polyline**.
- Pick **Draw/Polygon** and the command line will prompt

*Command: **_polygon** Enter number of sides <4>:*	***5***
Specify center of polygon or [Edge]:	***pick a point***
Enter an option [Inscribed in circle/Circumscribed about circle] <I>:	***i***
Specify radius of circle:	***450***

- Turn **Snap** off.
- Draw the plant with the **Polyline** command and the Planter should be similar to Figure 6.16.

***Figure 6.16**. The Planter drawn with Polygon and Polyline*

We are now ready to create **Blocks** of the symbols. We could have, of course, created a **Block** of each of the symbols directly after drawing each of them.

Creating Blocks of the Furniture Symbols

- Starting with the **Low Table** symbol create a **Block** of each of the symbols as described in Figure 6.1. The names of the **Blocks** are shown in Figure 6.17 along with the insertion points which are shown with an 'x'.

It is usual to pick an **insertion point** to be located somewhere on the block, the bottom left hand corner for example, but this will vary according to the type of drawing.
Where you see an **insertion point** just standing off the bottom left hand corner of a filletted or chamfered corner in Figure 6.17, it signifies the original corner before modifying to a fillet or chamfer. This is easily picked if you have created the blocks with **Snap On** as the cursor will jump to that point. **Erase** the symbols after making blocks - don't panic as you have stored them permanently in the drawing.

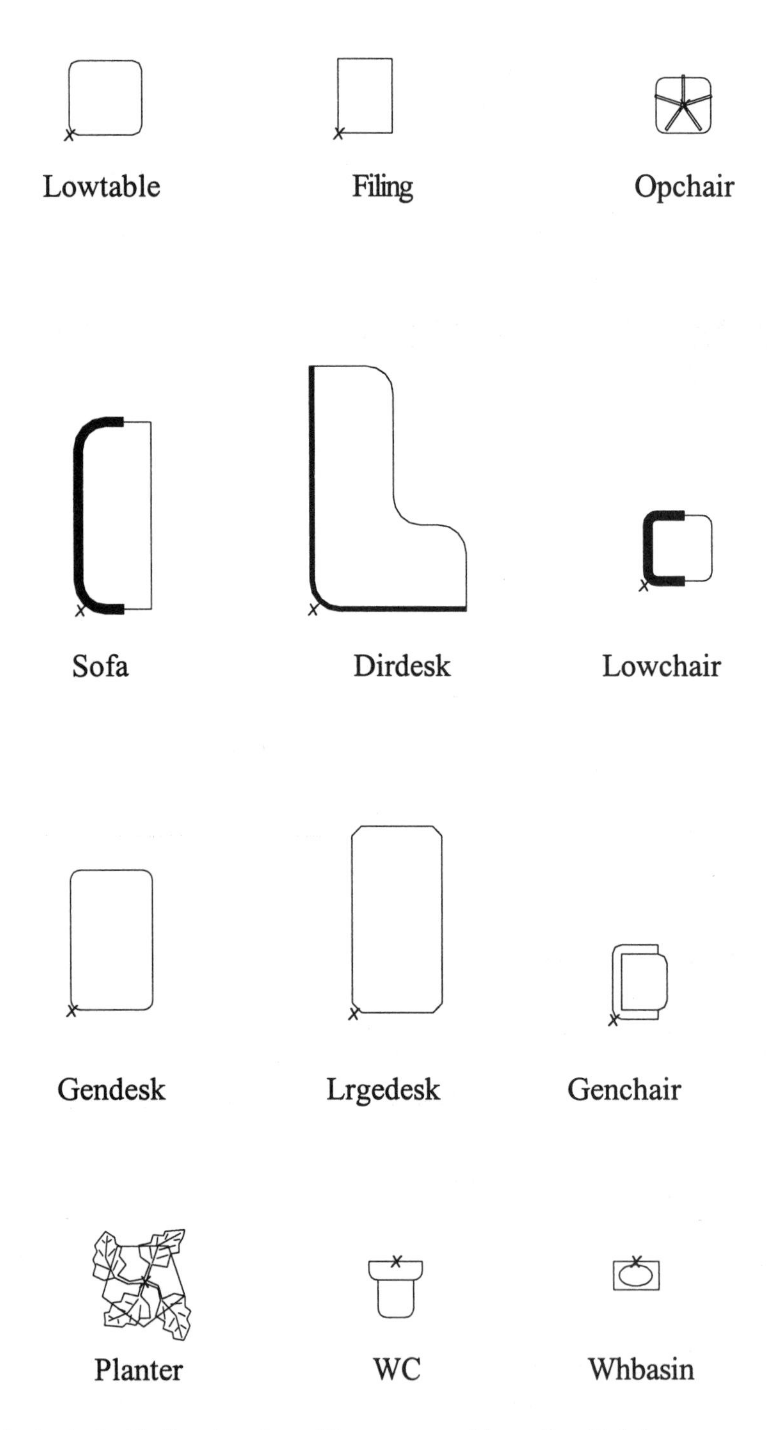

***Figure 6.17**. Blocks included in the drawing with names and Insertion Points*

Inserting the Blocks

- Make **Furniture** the **Current** layer. This is the destination layer for the blocks.
- Ensure that the **Doors** layer is **Thawed**.

- Pick the **Insert Block** button and the **Insert** dialogue box will appear as shown in Figure 6.18.

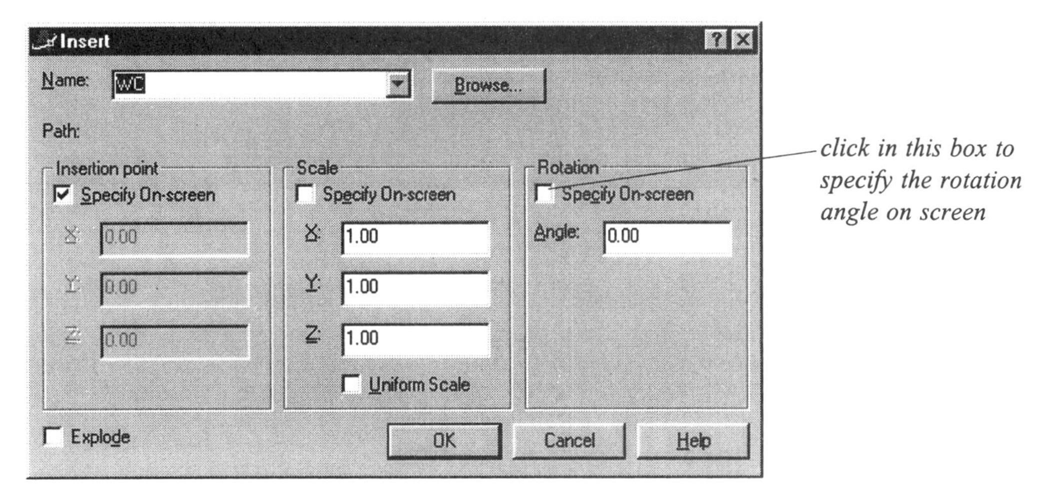

Figure 6.18 *The Insert dialogue box showing the WC block selected for insertion*

Your list of blocks in the pull-down menu should include all of the blocks just created.
You will need to place a check in the '**Specify On-screen**' box for the **Rotation Angle** of some of the **Blocks** as shown in Figure 6.18 because they will be inserted into the drawing at the same angle of rotation as they were drawn.

- Insert the **Blocks** as shown in Figure 6.19 or to your own design.

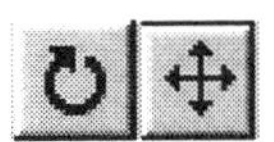

- You may need to **Move** and **Rotate** some the **Blocks** to locate them accurately.
- When you **Insert** the **Opchair Block** around the circular table, draw a **Circle** of 1000mm radius and **Modify/Polar Array** the chairs around it.

- To reduce the scale of the Planter, use **Insert/ Block** and the command line will prompt

  *Command: _**insert***

  Specify insertion point or [Scale/X/Y/Z/Rotate/PScale/PX/PY/PZ/PRotate]: ***s*** *(to scale the block)*

  Enter X scale factor, specify opposite corner, or [Corner/XYZ] <1>: ***.5*** *(scales the Block to half size)*

  Enter Y scale factor <use X scale factor>: ***Enter***

  Specify insertion point: ***pick*** *a point in the drawing (with Osnap if necessary)*

- Experiment by specifying a different **Yscale factor** from the **X scale factor** with the other blocks to see the result.

We have now completed the building interior as shown in Figure 6.19.

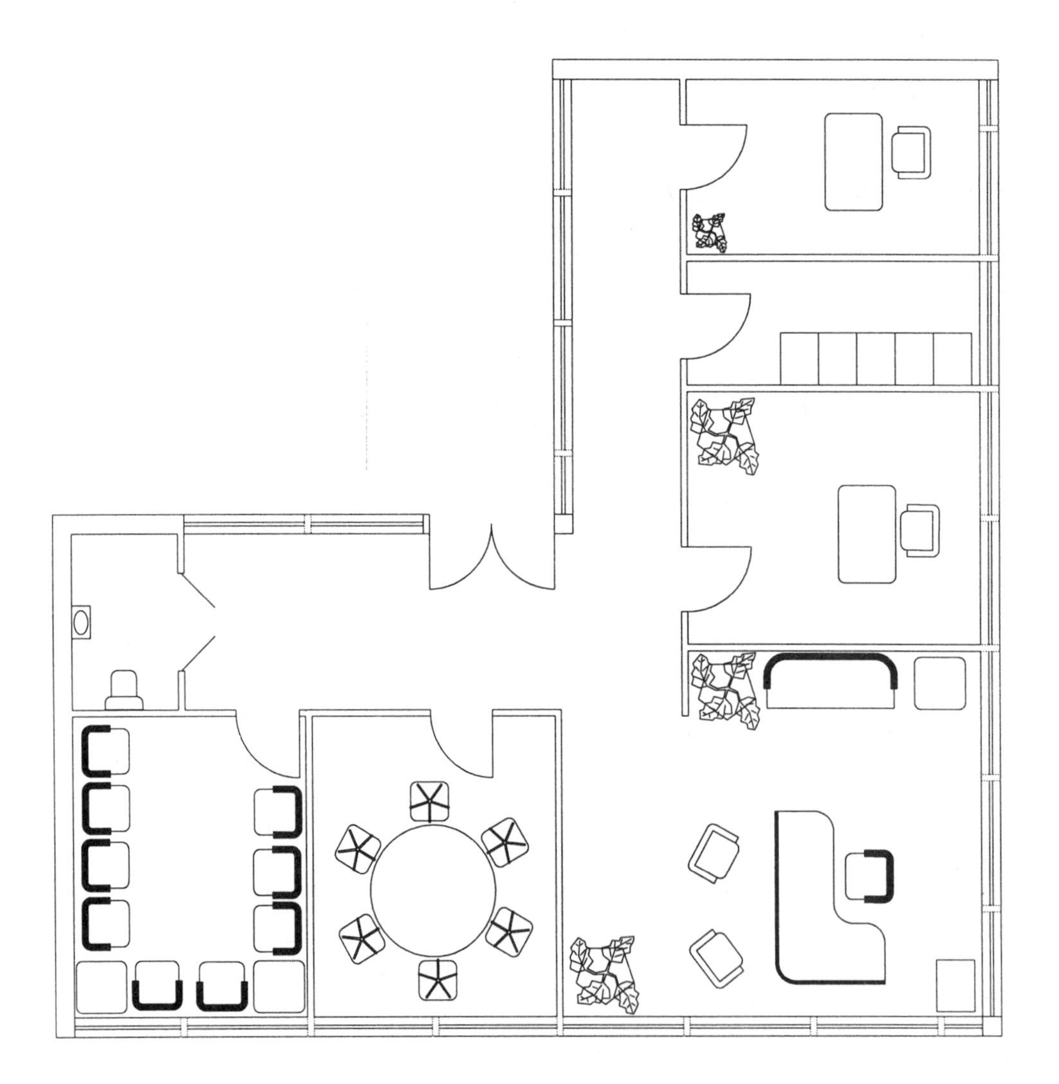

Figure 6.19*. The furniture Blocks in their positions.*

Chapter 7 — Drawing the Exterior Details

The exterior details include the boundary wall, patio, pond and driveway. We will also use a hatch pattern to simulate the paviors on the patio area.

Drawing the Boundary Wall

We will now draw the 500mm wide boundary wall with the **Multiline** command which draws a double line and caps the ends of the double line if it is specified.

- Create a layer called **Boundary** with a colour of your choice.
- Make **Boundary** the **Current** layer.
- **Freeze** the **Furniture** and **Doors** layers.
- From the **Format** pull-down menu use **Multiline Style** and the **Multiline Styles** dialogue box will appear as shown in Figure 7.1.

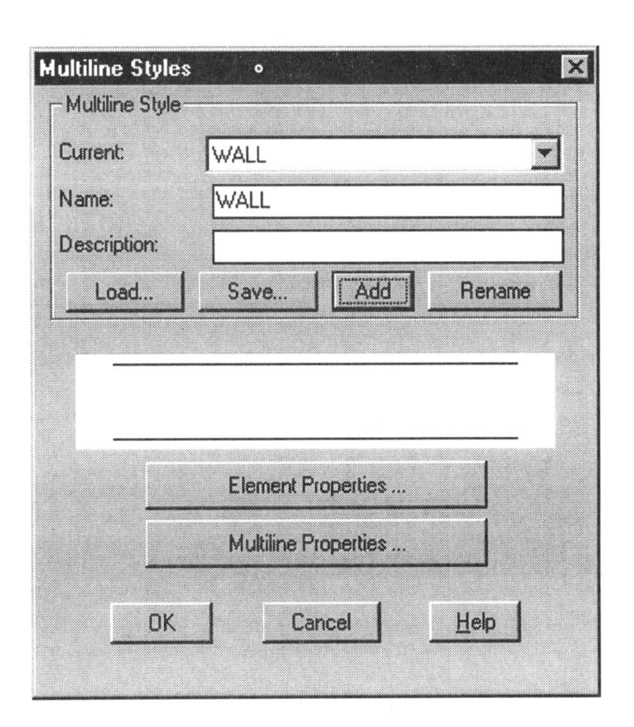

***Figure 7.1**. The Multiline Styles dialogue box with Wall as the Current style*

- **Name** the new style '**Wall**' by overtyping the name **Standard** in the **Name** box.
- Click on **Add** to make it the **Current** style as shown in Figure 7.1.
- To place caps at the end of the double line click on **Multiline Properties** and the **Multiline Properties** dialogue box overlays the previous and appears as shown in Figure 7.2.
- Put a check in the **Line Start** and **End** boxes.
- Click **OK**.
- The **Multiline Styles** dialogue box reappears.

Note that the depiction of the style now has endcaps.

- Click **OK** in the **Multiline Properties** dialogue box.

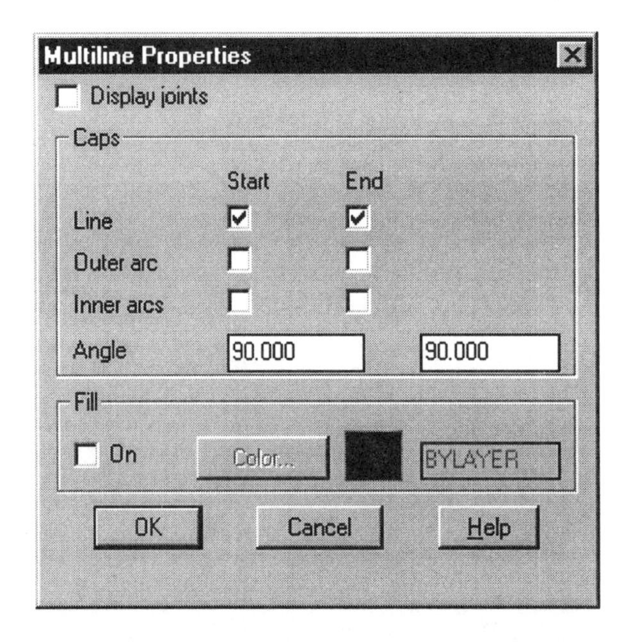

***Figure 7.2**. The Multiline Properties dialogue box with Caps at Start and End*

To draw the wall we will use **Absolute coordinates**.

- Pick **Draw/Multiline** and the command line will prompt

Command: ***_mline***

Current settings: Justification = Top, Scale = 20.00, Style = WALL

Specify start point or [Justification/Scale/STyle]:	*s*
Enter mline scale <20.00>:	***500*** *(sets the wall width to 500mm)*

Current settings: Justification = Top, Scale = 500.00, Style = WALL

Specify start point or [Justification/Scale/STyle]:	***2000,24250***
Specify next point:	***28250,24250***
Specify next point or [Undo]:	***28250,750***
Specify next point or [Close/Undo]:	***1750,750***
Specify next point or [Close/Undo]:	***1750,19000***
Specify next point or [Close/Undo]:	***Enter***

The drawing should now look like that shown in Figure 7.3.

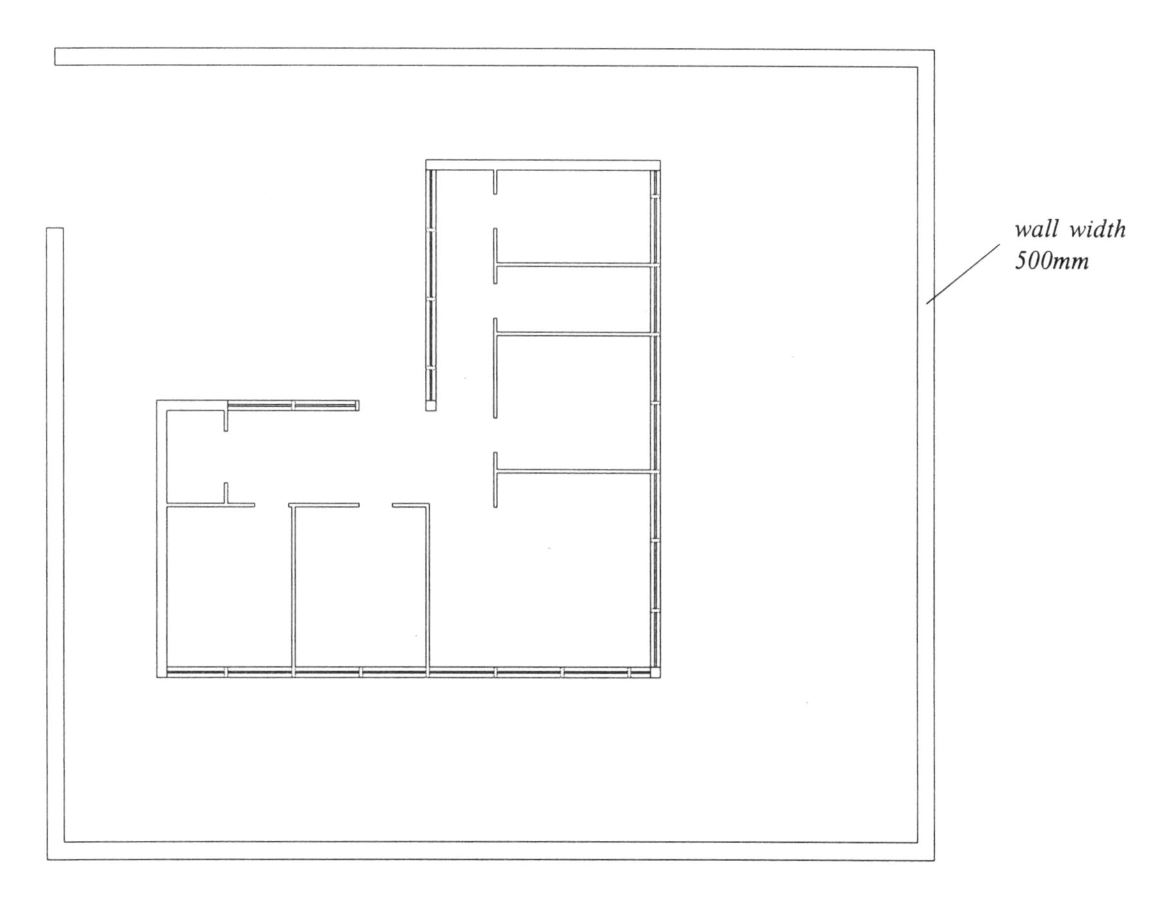

Figure 7.3*. The completed Boundary Wall drawn with Multiline*

To make the wall more realistic, a height of approximately 500-750mm could be added to the wall as shown in Chapter 2, Figure 2.2. If you do this, remember that you must use the **Chprop** command to change the **Thickness** (which is what AutoCAD calls height).
Remember, also, that when using the **Thickness** command the top of the boundary wall will not appear solid until 3Dfaces have been applied. We use the **3DFace** command later in the book when the roof is constructed, so I suggest you gain the **3DFace** command skills on the roof first and return to the boundary wall later.

Drawing the Driveway

We can now draw the driveway at the entrance to the site using the **Arc/3Points** comand. This command allows us to specify a start and end of the first arc and the third point is dragged into position to form the arc visually.

- Create a layer called **Driveway** with a colour of your choice and make it the **Current** layer.
- From the **Draw/Arc** pull-down menu pick **3Points** and the command line will prompt

*Command: _**arc** Specify start point of arc or [CEnter]:* *_endp of* ***(pick** as shown in Figure 7.4)*
Specify second point of arc or [CEnter/ENd]: ***(pick** as shown in Figure 7.4)*
Specify end point of arc: *_endp of* ***(pick** as shown in Figure 7.4)*

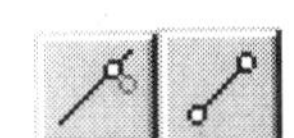

- Repeat for the second arc as shown in Figure 7.4 using the **Start, End, Direction** option picking the **Nearest** for the first point and the **Endpoint** for the second and dragging the arc into position for the **Direction**.

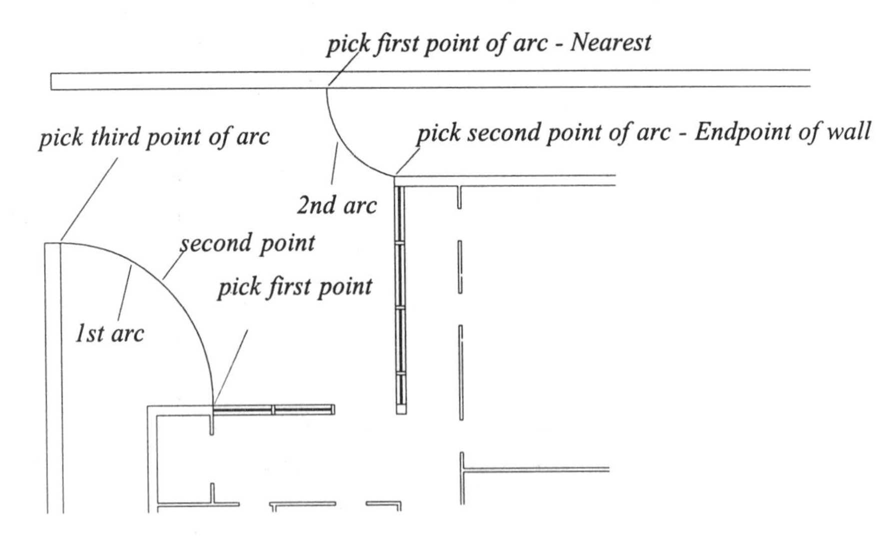

***Figure 7.4**. Using the Arc command to draw the driveway*

Drawing the Patio Edge

The edge of the patio can be drawn using a combination of **Polylines** and **Polyarcs**. Why are we going to use **Polyline** to do this? It is easier to pick when we fill the area with a hatch pattern.

- Make **Patioedge** the **Current** layer.

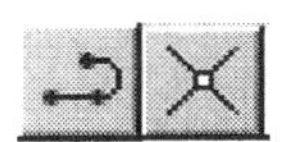

- Pick the **Draw/Polyline** button and the command line will prompt

  *Command: **_pline***

  Specify start point: *_int of* *(**pick** the building as shown in Figure 7.5)*

  Current line-width is 0.0000

  *Specify next point or [Arc/Close/Halfwidth/Length/Undo/Width]: **a** (for arc)*

  Specify endpoint of arc or [Angle/CEnter/CLose/Direction/Halfwidth/Line/Radius/Second pt/Undo/Width]:

  *(**pick** a point as shown in Figure 7.5)*

  Specify endpoint of arc or[Angle/CEnter/CLose/Direction/Halfwidth/Line/Radius/Second pt/Undo/Width]:

  *(**pick** a point as shown in Figure 7.5)*

  Specify endpoint of arc or[Angle/CEnter/CLose/Direction/Halfwidth/Line/Radius/Second pt/Undo/Width]:

  ***_int** of (**pick** as shown in Figure 7.5)*

- Draw as many **Polyline arcs** as you feel necessary to complete the edge of the patio in between the **Intersections** of the building corners. Complete the pond outline as shown in Figure 7.5.

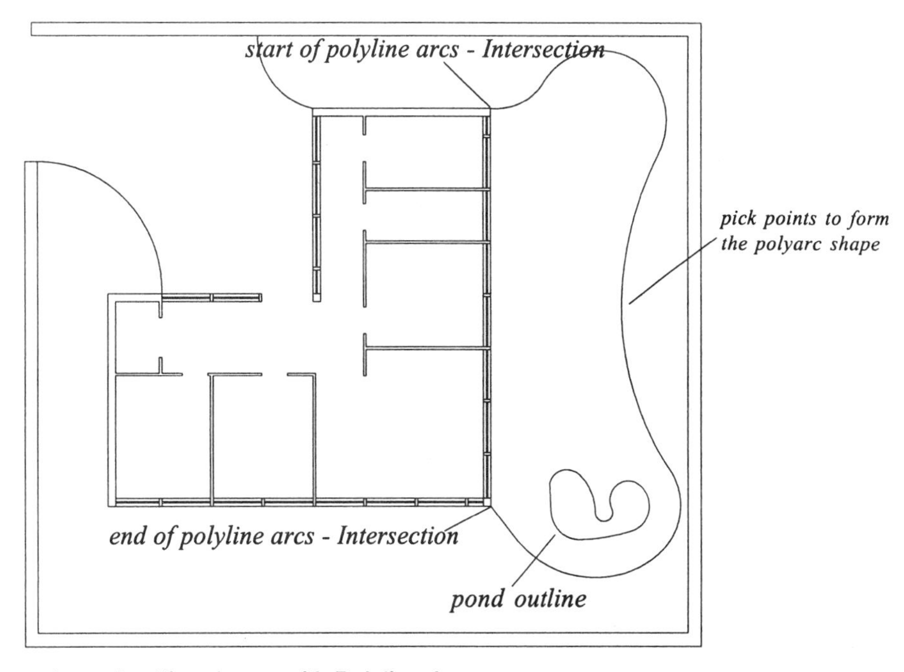

***Figure 7.5**. The patio and pond outline drawn with Polyline Arcs*

Using a Hatch Pattern for the Patio

Hatching fills a specified area in a drawing with a pattern that is predefined or one that you can create. We will use a predefined pattern.

- Make **PatioHatch** layer the **Current** layer.

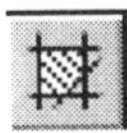

- Pick the **Draw/Hatch** button and the **Boundary Hatch** dialogue box will appear as shown in Figure 7.6.
- Click on the **Pattern** scroll bar and select the **AR-Hbone** style as shown in Figure 7.6.
- Click on **Pick Points** and the dialogue box disappears and the command line will prompt

  *Command: **_bhatch***

  Select internal point: Selecting everything... ***click** within the patio boundary*

  Selecting everything visible...

  Analyzing the selected data...

  Analyzing internal islands...

  Select internal point: ***Enter***

The dialogue box reappears.

- You can now either look at the hatch pattern in situ with **Preview** or you can **OK** the pattern.
- **Preview** gives the opportunity to change the pattern and scale for example before finally clicking on **OK**.
- Changing the **Scale** to anything between say, 25 and 50 will give a less dense pattern, but choose your own.

- If clicking on **Pick Points** gives a **'Valid hatch boundary not found'** message, use the **Select Objects** button to pick the patio outline, the building line and the pond outline.

Figure 7.7 shows the completed patio area after hatching.

Two-dimensional drawing is now complete. We can now start annotating the drawing with dimensions and text.

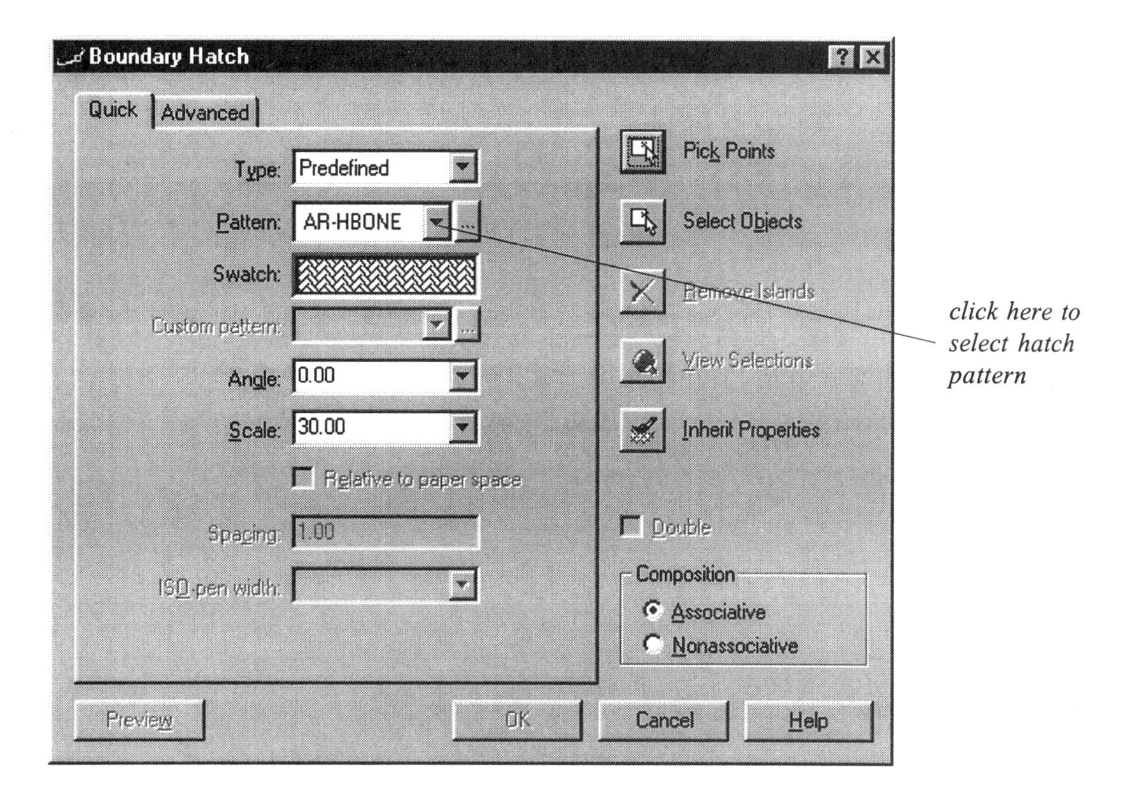

***Figure 7.6**. The Boundary Hatch dialogue box*

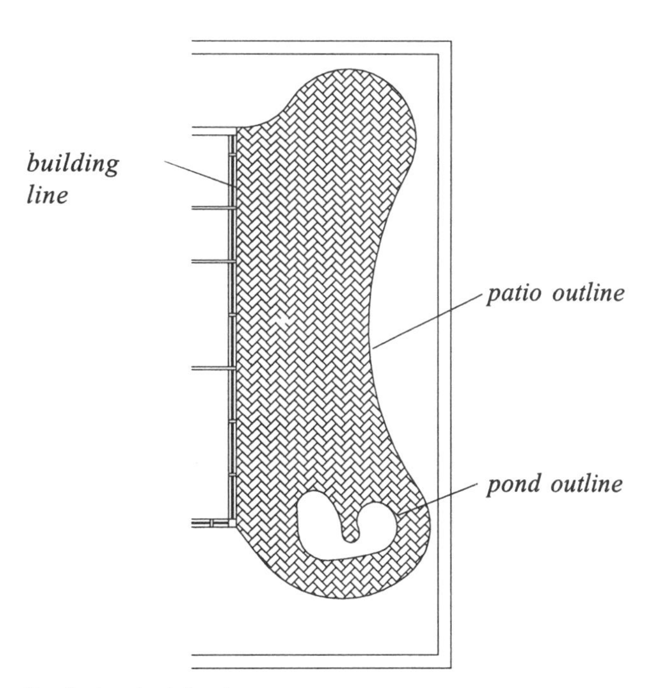

***Figure 7.7**. The patio after being hatched*

Chapter 8 — Dimensioning and Annotating the Drawing

Before dimensioning the drawing we need to set up the style and method of dimensioning through the **Format/Dimension Styles** pull-down menu. We will save our own dimension style through the **Lines and Arrows, Text** and **Fit** tabs with values as shown in Figure 8.1.

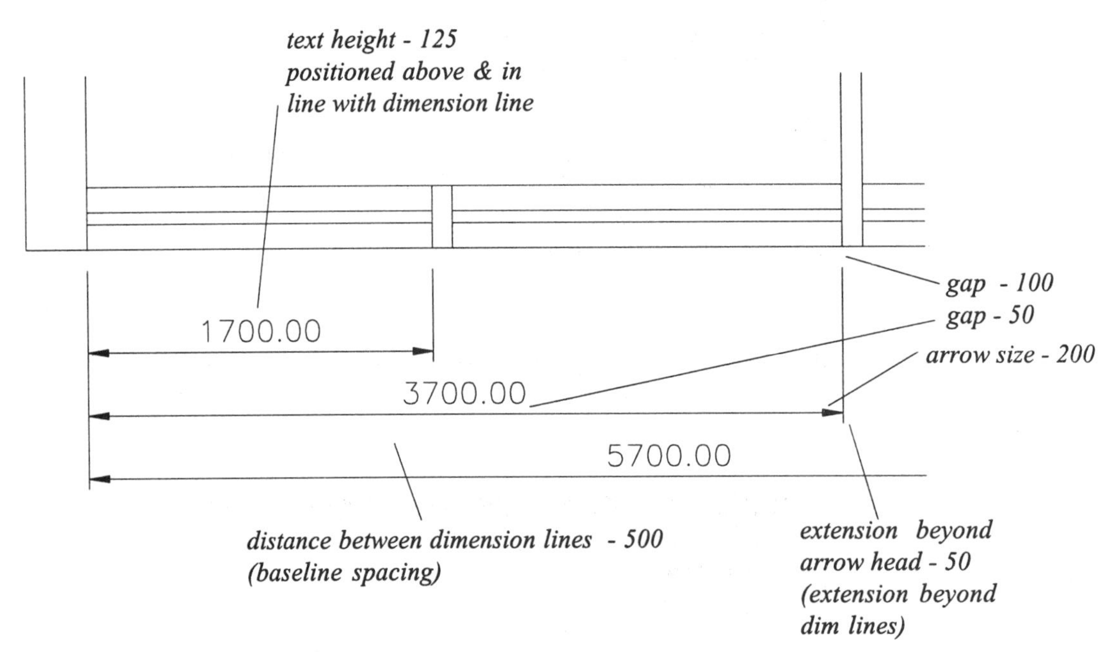

Figure 8.1. *Dimension style details*

Setting up the Dimension Style

■ Pick the **Format/Dimension Styles** pull-down menu and the **Dimension Style Manager** dialogue box will appear as shown in Figure 8.2.

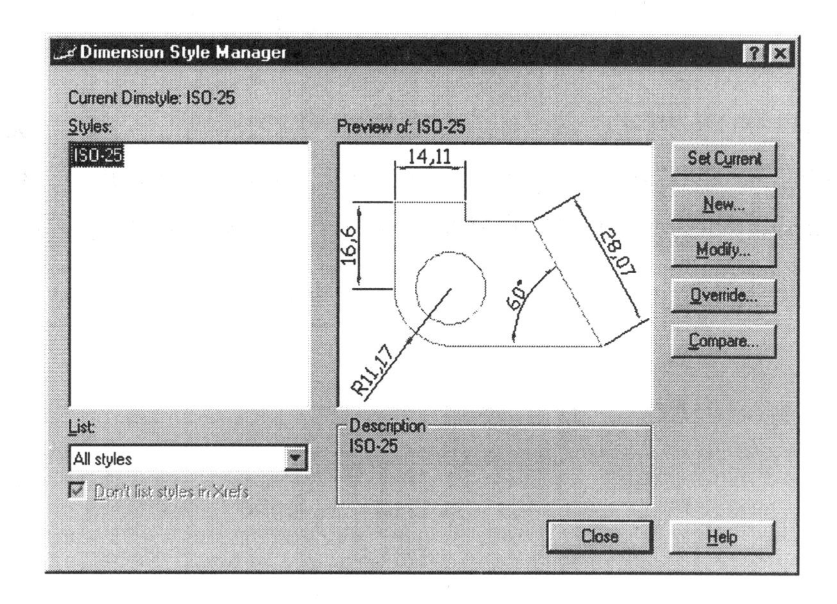

__Figure 8.2__. The Dimension Style Manager dialogue box

■ Pick the **Modify** button and in the **Lines and Arrows** tab enter the values highlighted in Figure 8.3.

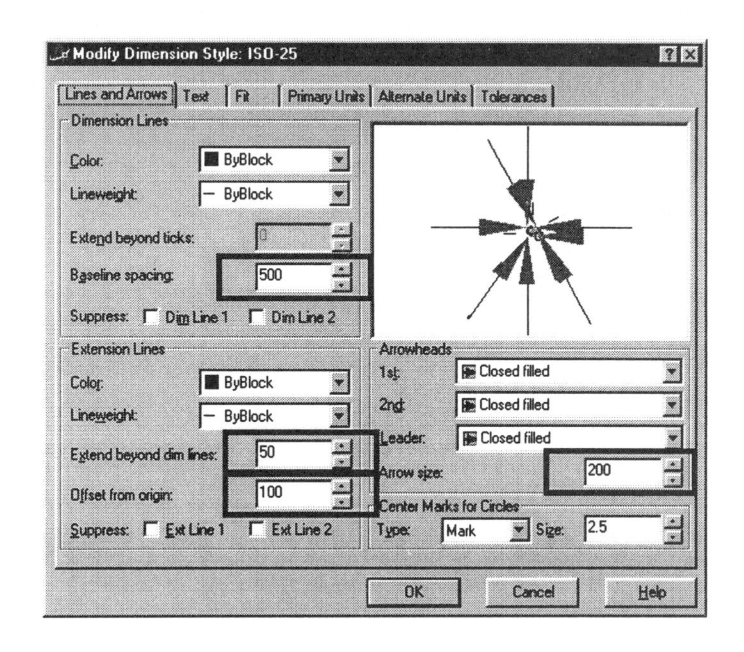

__Figure 8.3__. The Modify Dimension Style/Lines and Arrows dialogue box

■ Click on the **Text** tab and enter as highlighted in Figure 8.4.

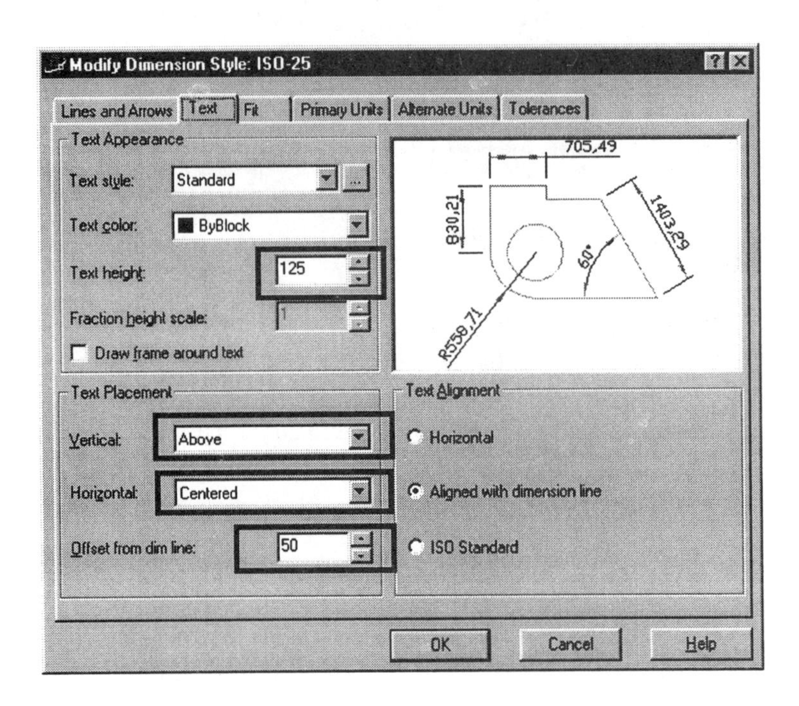

Figure 8.4. The Modify Dimension Style/Text dialogue box

■ Click on the **Fit** tab and enter as highlighted in Figure 8.5.

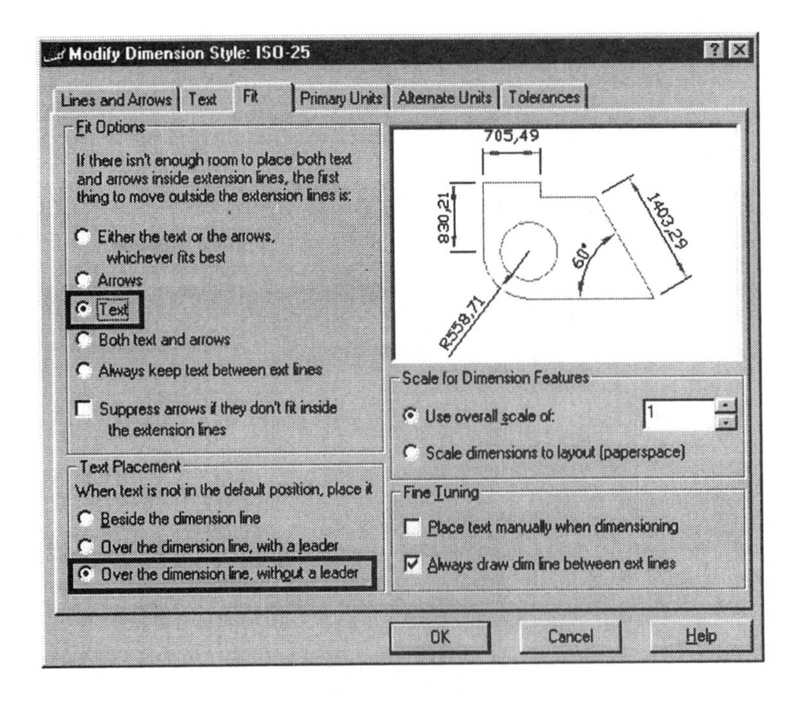

Figure 8.5. The Modify/Dimension Style/Fit dialogue box

- Click on **OK**.
- The **Dimension Style Manager** dialogue box reappears.
- Save the new dimension style by clicking on **New**.

The **Create New Dimension Style** dialogue box will appear as shown in Figure 8.6.

- Enter the **New Style Name** of **Dimdetail**.

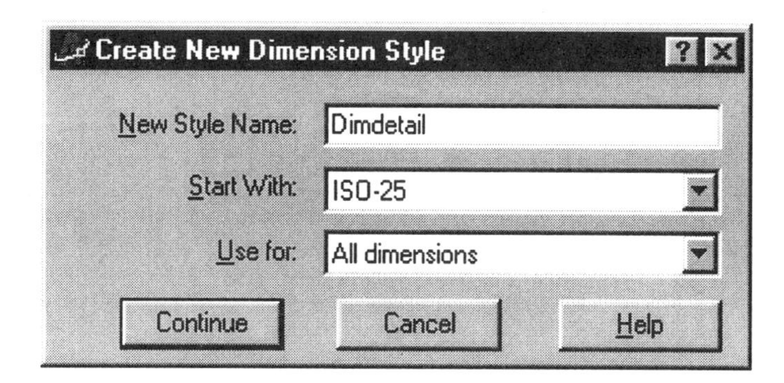

***Figure 8.6**. The Create New Dimension Style dialogue box*

- Click on **Continue**.

The name of the new style will appear in the **Styles** window of the **Dimension Styles Manager** dialogue box.

- Click on the new name **Dimdetail**.
- Click on **Set Current**.
- Click on **Close**.

We are now ready to dimension the drawing.

Dimensioning the Drawing

- Pick the **View/Toolbars** pull-down menu to load the **Dimension** toolbar as shown in Figure 8.7. Position it conveniently on your screen.

Figure 8.7. The Dimension toolbar

- Make the **Dimensions** layer the **Current** layer.
- **Freeze** the **Doors** layer.

- **Pan** or **Zoom** to the bottom left corner of the building as shown in Figure 8.8.

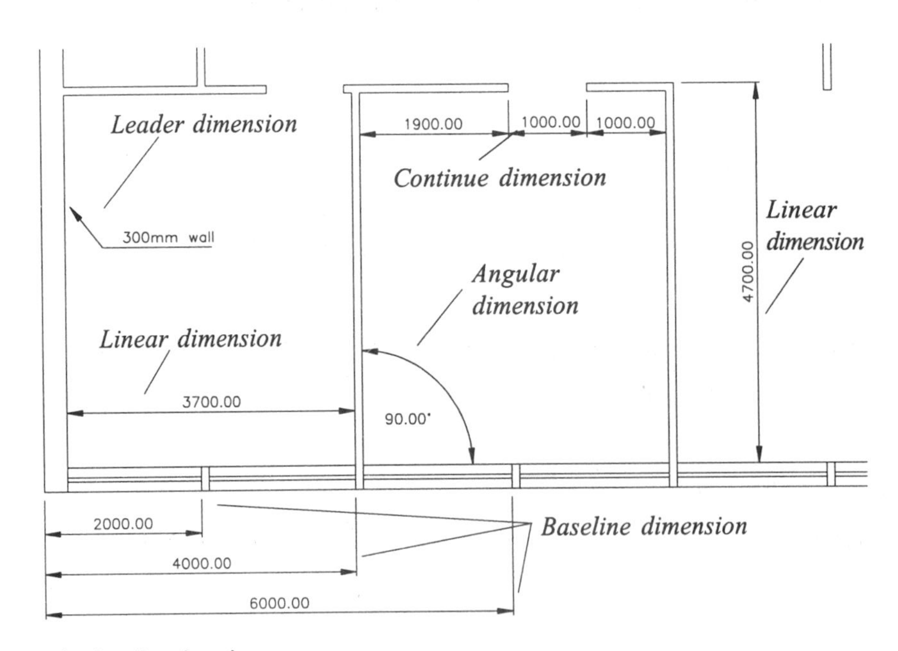

Figure 8.8. Dimensioning the drawing

Linear Dimensions

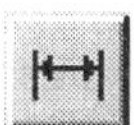

- Pick the **Linear Dimension** button.
- Draw the **3700.00** width dimension of the room by using the **Intersections** of the walls and windows as shown in Figure 8.8.
- Follow the command line prompts.

AutoCAD also allows you to dimension a line by simply picking it and pressing **Enter** instead of using a selection method.
Try it by picking the window wall of the **3700.00** dimension and the command line will prompt

Command:	***_dimlinear***
Specify first extension line origin or <select object>:	***Enter***
Select object to dimension:	***pick** the window wall*
Specify dimension line location or [Mtext/Text/Angle/Horizontal/Vertical/Rotated]:	***drag** the dimension to a suitable location*
Dimension text = 3700.00	***Enter***

- Repeat the **Linear Dimension** for the **4700.00** dimension.

Baseline Dimensions

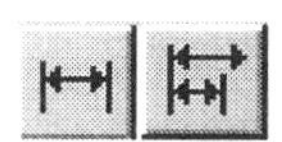

- For the dimensions outside of the building (**2000.00, 4000.00** and **6000.00**) use the **Linear Dimension** button to measure and position the 2000.00 dimension.
- To create a baseline dimension pick the **Baseline Dimension** button and the the command line will prompt you for another second point, using the first point chosen as the datum of the dimension.

*Command: **_dimlinear***

Specify first extension line origin or <select object>:	***_endp** of external corner*
Specify second extension line origin:	***_endp** of 1st mullion line as shown in Figure 8.8*
Specify dimension line location or [Mtext/Text/Angle/Horizontal/Vertical/Rotated]:	***pick** location*

Dimension text = 2000.00

Command: _dimbaseline

*Specify a second extension line origin or [Undo/Select] <Select>: **_endp** of 2nd mullion line*

Dimension text = 4000.00

Specify a second extension line origin or [Undo/Select] <Select>: _**endp** *of 3rd mullion line*

Dimension text = 6000.00

Specify a second extension line origin or [Undo/Select] <Select>: ***Enter***

Select base dimension: ***Enter***

You will see that the 3 dimensions are automatically separated by a spacing of 500 which we set in the **Lines and Arrows/Baseline Spacing** tab.

Continue Dimensions

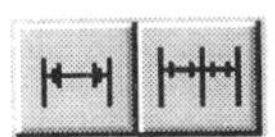

- Using the **Continue Dimension** button to draw in the 1900.00, 1000.00 and 1000.00 dimensons as shown in Figure 8.8.
- Follow the command line prompts.

Dimension Text Editing

- Use the **Dimension Text Edit** button to move the 1000.00 figures to a position of your choice.

Angular Dimensions

- Use the **Angular Dimension** button to measure the wall angle with the text inside the dimension arc as shown in Figure 8.8.
- Follow the command line prompts.

Leader Text Dimensions

- For the wall width description use the **Quick Leader** button and enter the text at the command line prompt as shown in Figure 8.8.

Practise dimensioning the drawing with dimensions as shown in Figure 8.10.

Setting the Text Style

Before adding text to the drawing we must first set up a text style in a similar way to the methods of setting a dimension style. We will set up the same text style as the dimensioning style — **Roman Simplex** with a height of 200.

- Pick the **Format/Text Style** pull-down menu and the **Text Style** dialogue box will appear as shown in Figure 8.9.
- Change to the values highlighted.
- Click on **Apply**.
- Click on **Close**.

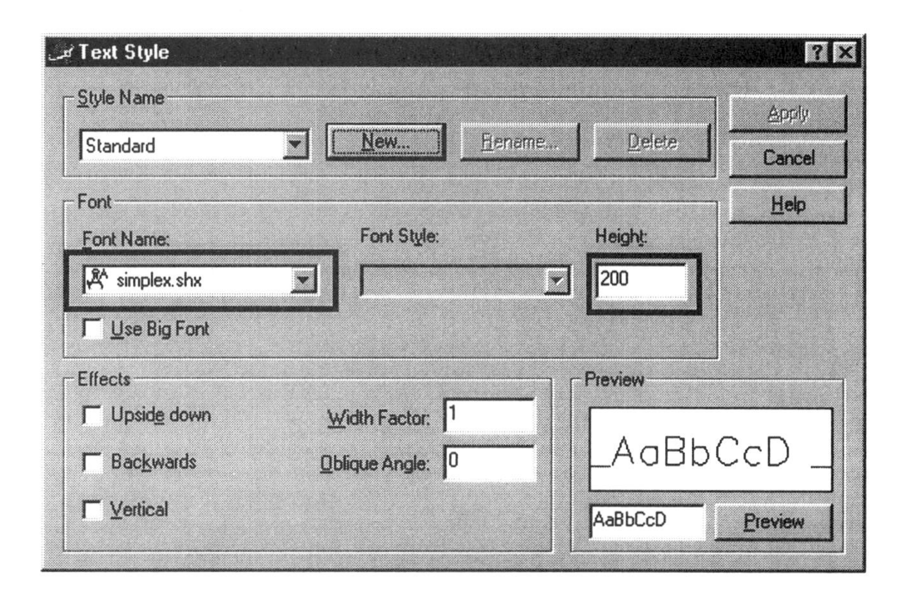

Figure 8.9. *The Text Style dialogue box.*

Adding Text to the Drawing

- Set the **Current** layer to **Text**.
- **Thaw** the **Furniture** layer.
- Use the **Draw/Text/Single Line Text** pull-down menu and the command line will prompt

Command: _dtext

Current text style: "Standard" Text height: 200.0000

Specify start point of text or [Justify/Style]:	***pick** a point in the drawing as shown in Figure 8.10*
Specify rotation angle of text <0>:	***Enter***
Enter text:	***Finance Director***
Enter text:	***Enter***
Enter text:	***Enter***

This will place the words **Finance Director** in the drawing.

- Repeat this for the remainder of the drawing text as shown in Figure 8.10.

- **Thaw** all layers.

- Pick **Zoom/Extents** from the **Zoom** pull-down menu and view the drawing.

The 2D drawing is now complete as shown in the target drawing Figure 8.10.

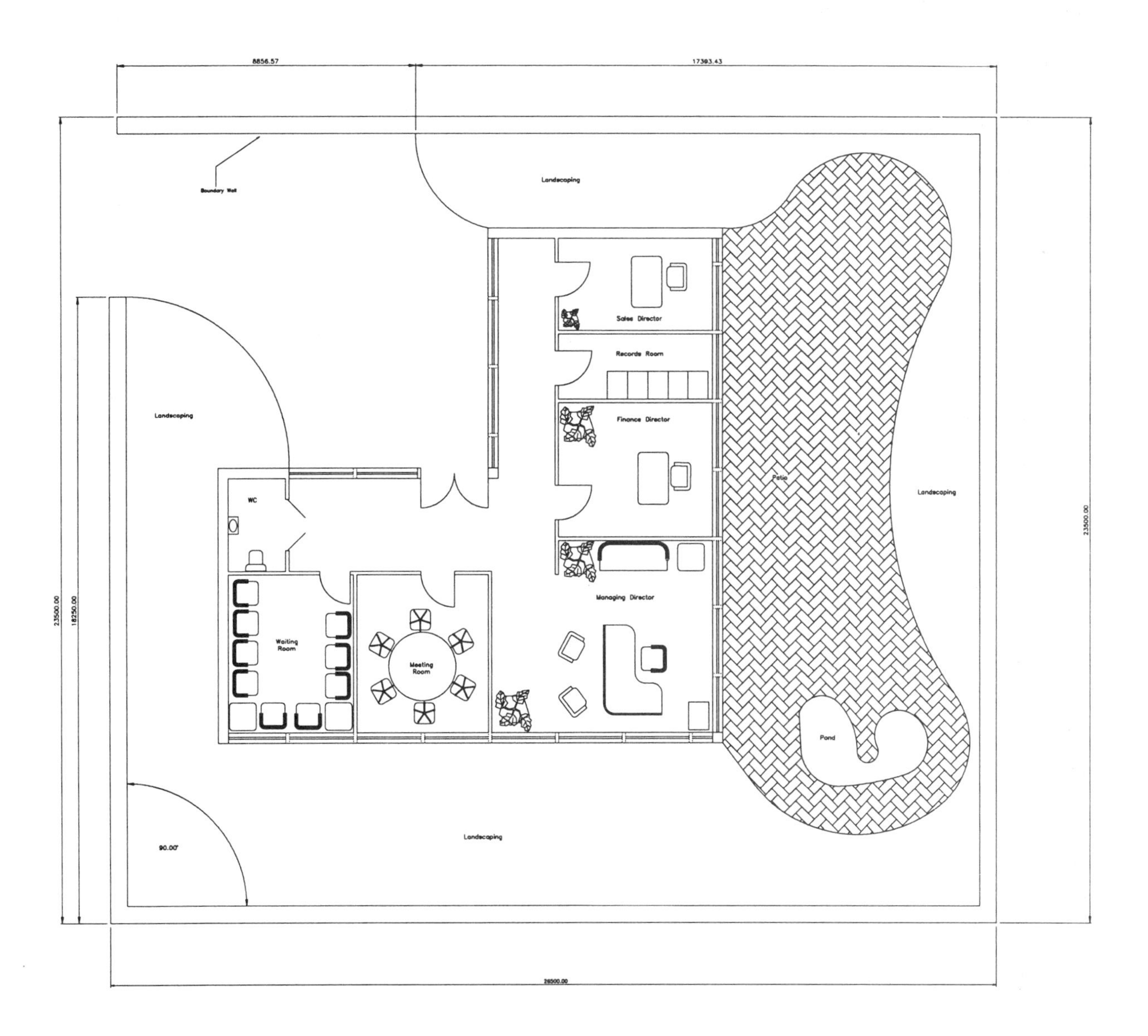

***Figure 8.10**. The 2D plan target drawing showing dimensions and description text*

Chapter 9 — Changing the View of the Drawing

So far we have worked and drawn in 2D i.e. looking from directly above the drawing in a planimetric view. To make it easier to change objects from 2D to 3D we shall view the drawing initially from a **SE isometric** viewpoint.

We shall change the end walls, internal partitions and the mullion heights to 2800mm and the walls between the mullions to 700mm to form low sills.

- Make the **Roof** layer **Current**.
- **Freeze** all layers except for the **Roof, Walls and Windows**.

- From the **View/Toolbars** pull-down menu load the **View** toolbar.
- Pick the **SE Isometric** button and the drawing will appear as shown in Figure 9.1.

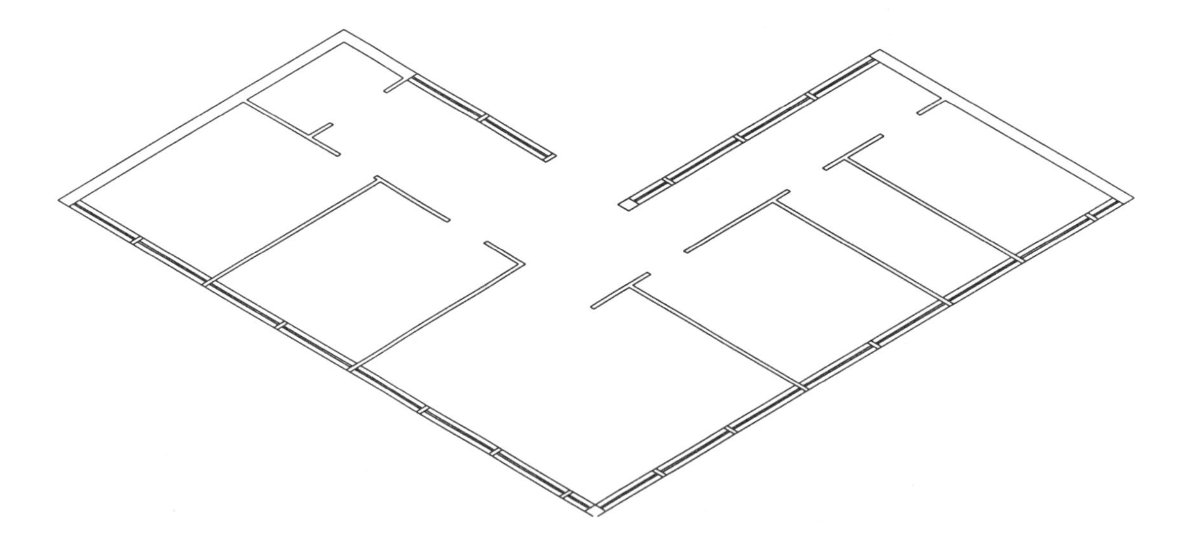

***Figure 9.1**. A SE Isometric view.*

Creating 3D from 2D

To change the height of the end walls, internal partitions and the mullions to 2800mm and the walls between the mullions to 700mm we will use the **Chprop/Thickness** command to give height to selected objects in the drawing.

- Type **Chprop** at the command line

Command: ***chprop***

Select objects: Specify opposite corner: 78 found ***(pick** the objects to change — your number may be different)*

Select objects: ***Enter***

Enter property to change [Color/LAyer/LType/ltScale/LWeight/Thickness]: ***th*** (for thickness)

Specify new thickness <0.0000>: ***2800***

Enter property to change [Color/LAyer/LType/ltScale/LWeight/Thickness]: ***Enter***

Another method, but with the same result is from the **Modify Properties** toolbar.

- Pick **Properties** and the properties dialogue box will appear as shown in Figure 9.2.
- Change the **Thickness** value to 2800 as shown.
- With the dialogue box still active (visible on screen), select the objects to change.
- **Grips** will appear on the objects — small blue squares on the objects.
- Close the dialogue box.
- Press **Esc** twice to clear the **Grips** and the thickness of the objects will be changed.

Using either method, repeat the operation for the walls between the mullions but with a **Thickness** of 700mm.

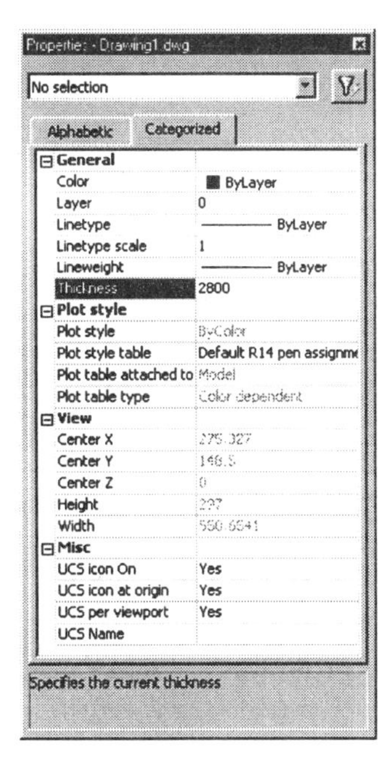

Figure 9.2*. The Properties dialogue box*

Making the Drawing look Solid

When you have completed changing the **Thickness** your drawing will appear as a 'wire-frame' with normally invisible lines being visible as shown in Figure 9.3.

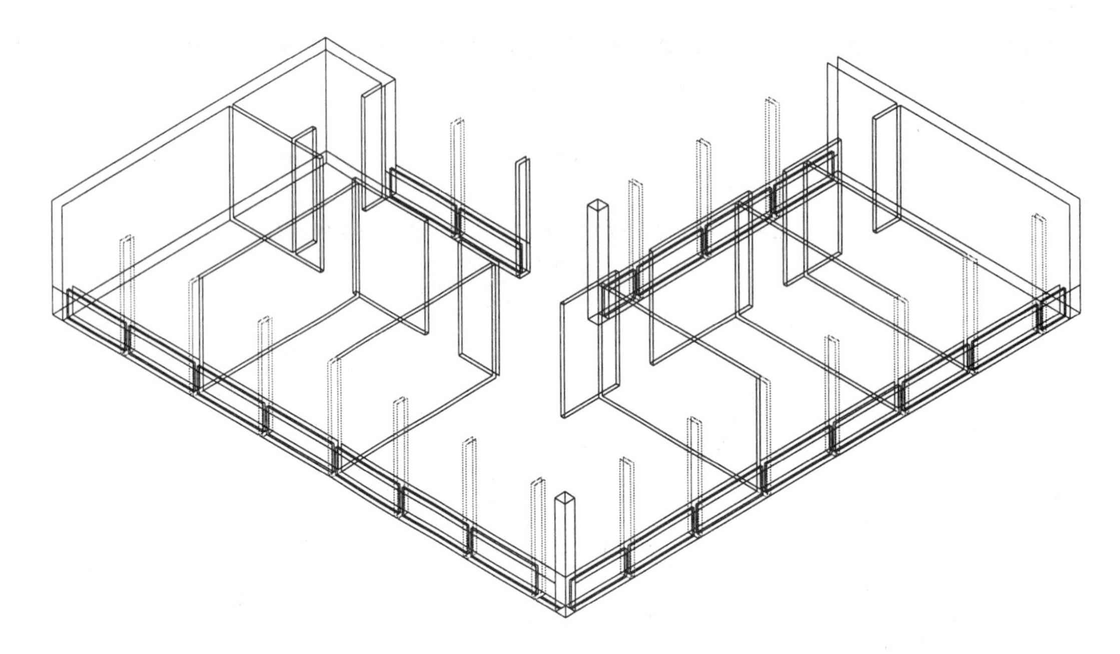

Figure 9.3. The building after the Thickness command.

- To make the drawing appear solid use the **Hide** command from the **View** pull-down menu and the drawing will appear as shown in Figure 9.4.

When you change your view, either by **Pan** or **Zoom** for example, you will need to use **Hide** to produce a solid view.

We are now ready to draw the outline of the roof.

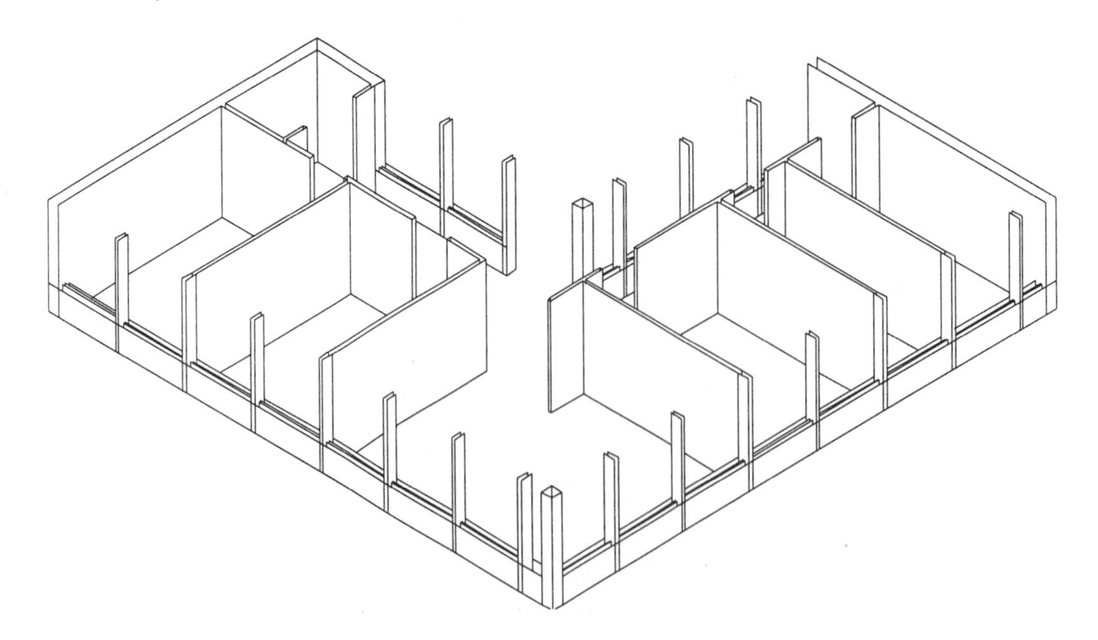

Figure 9.4. The solid building after the Hide command.

To Draw the Roof

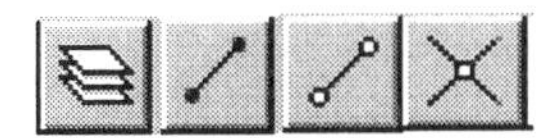

- Ensure that the Roof layer is **Current**.
- **Draw** a line around the perimeter of the building picking the **Endpoints** or **Intersections** of the corners as shown in Figure 9.5.

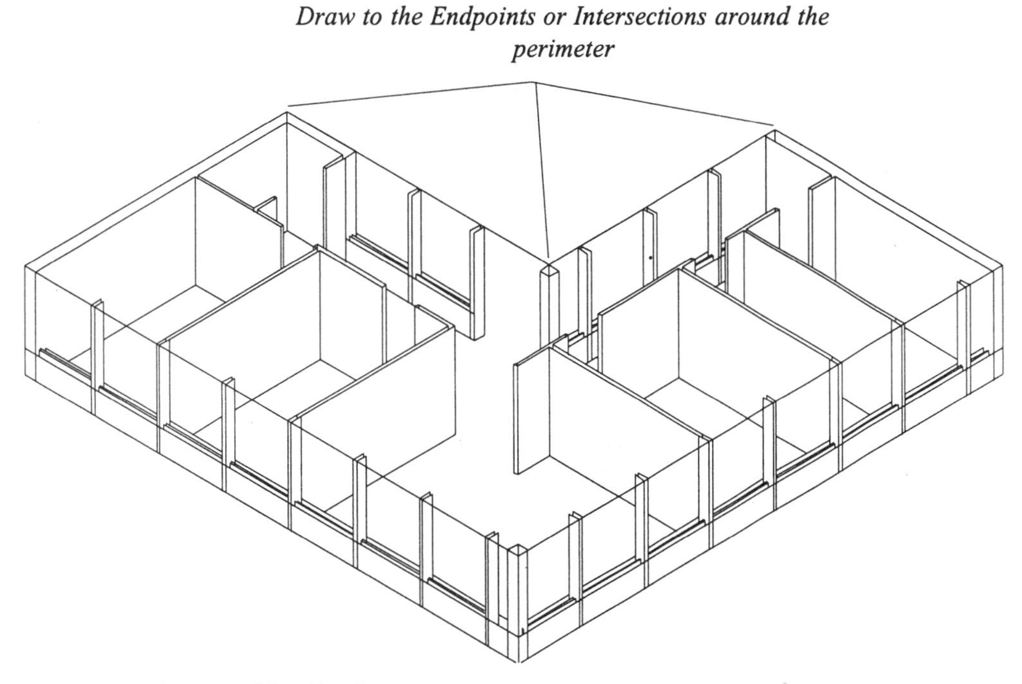

Figure 9.5. *The perimeter of the Roof*

Drawing with 3D Coordinates

So far we have used 2-dimensional coordinates X and Y, to draw the objects in the drawing. 3-Dimensional coordinates include Z so that the coordinates become X,Y, Z where Z is the height from base level. We have just changed the Z value of the walls and mullions.
We will use X, Y, Z **absolute coordinates** to draw the ridge line of the roof.

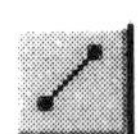

- Pick the **Draw** button and the command line will prompt

Command: _line Specify first point:	***5000,10000, 5600***
Specify next point or [Undo]:	***16500, 10000, 5600***
Specify next point or [Undo]:	***16500, 21000, 5600***
Specify next point or [Close/Undo]:	***Enter***

and the drawing will look like Figure 9.6.

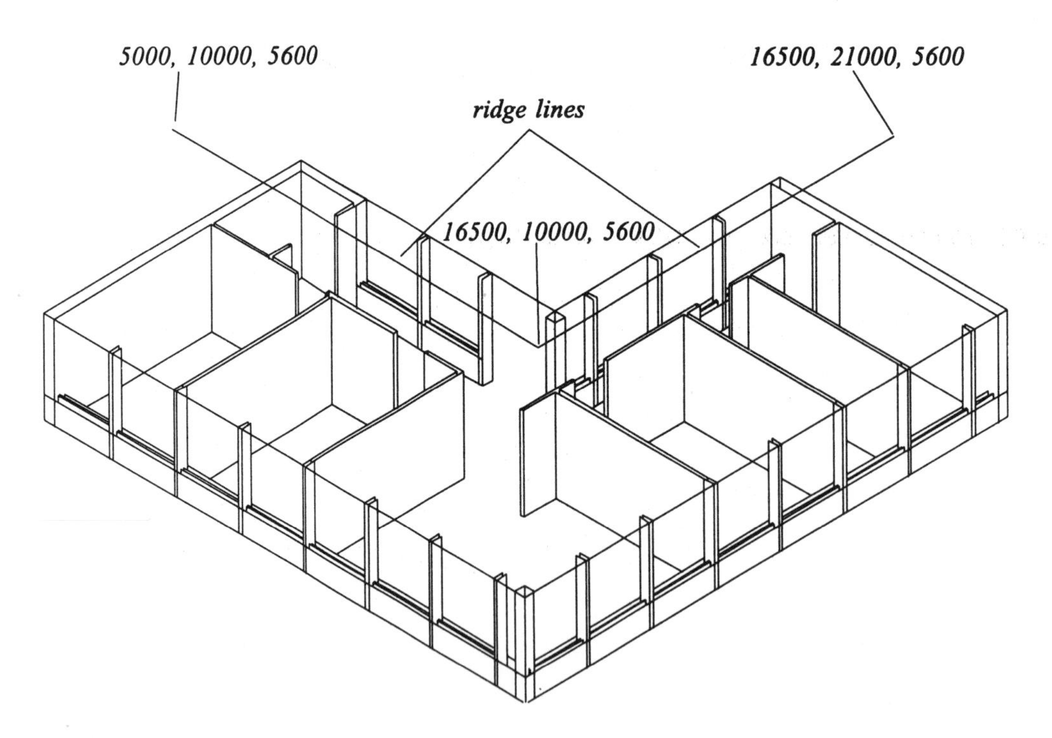

Figure 9.6*. The drawn ridge line*

- **Freeze** all layers except for the **Roof** layer.

- To complete the roof, **Draw** the gable ends and the hips as shown in Figure 9.7 using the **Endpoints** or **Intersections** of the previously drawn roof lines.

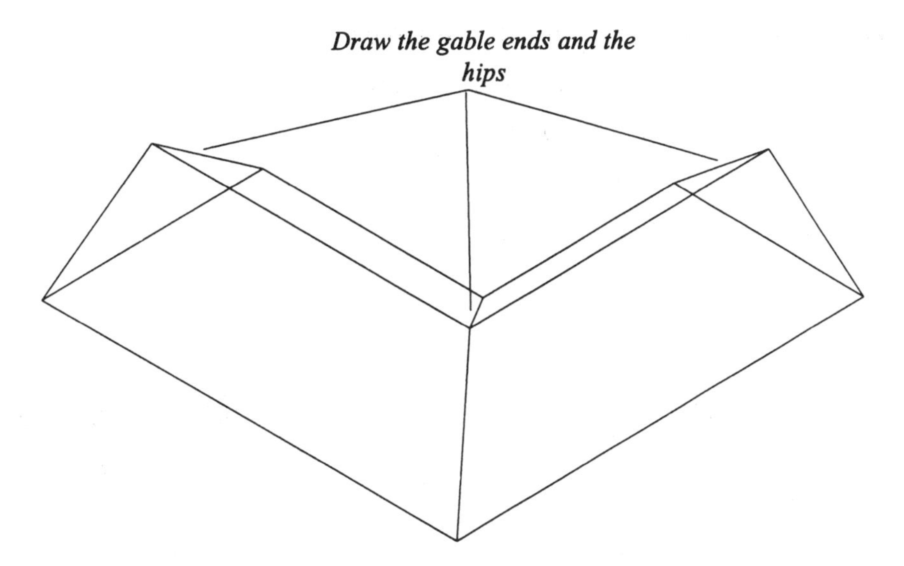

***Figure 9.7.** The completed roof with gable ends and hips*

Making the Roof Solid

We have created the roof by simply joining lines together in 3D space. The roof will not present a solid appearance like the walls until a surface is applied. (The wall surfaces were applied automatically with the **Thickness** command).

We will use the **3DFace** command to apply an invisible surface or skin to the different roof planes so that when we use the **Hide** command it will appear solid. The second reason for doing this is that when we apply a **Hatch** to appear as roof tiles the hatching will not appear 'see-through'.

Prior to hatching the drawing plane will be changed from a **World Coordinate System (WCS)** to a **User Coordinate System (UCS)** whose position in 3D space can be saved.

- Create a layer called **3DFace** with a colour of your choice.
- Make **3DFace** the **Current** layer.

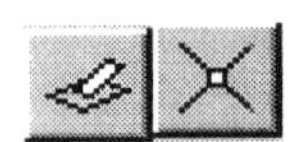

- From the **View/Toolbars** pull-down menu load the **Surfaces** toolbar.
- Click on the **3DFace** button and the command line will prompt

*Command: **3dface***	
Specify first point or [Invisible]: _int of	***pick** as shown in Figure 9.8*
Specify second point or [Invisible]: _int of	***pick** as shown in Figure 9.8*
Specify third point or [Invisible] <exit>: _int of	***pick** as shown in Figure 9.8*
*Specify fourth point or [Invisible] <create three-sided face>: **_int of***	***pick** as shown in Figure 9.8*
Specify third point or [Invisible] <exit>:	***Enter***

- Repeat this for all the surfaces of the roof including the gable ends which are triangular in shape and have only 3 **Intersection** pick points, not 4.
- Close the **Surfaces** toolbar when complete.

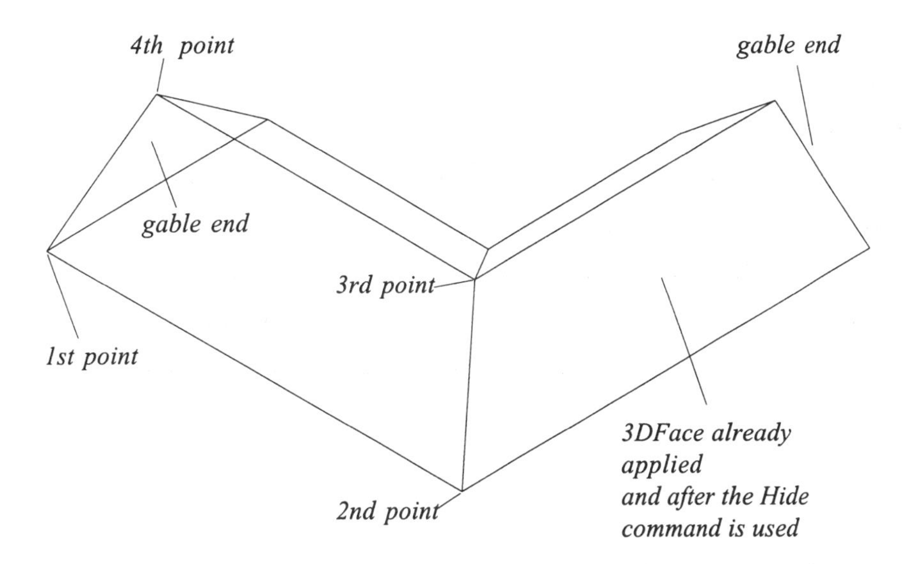

***Figure 9.8**. The results of the 3DFace command*

Changing to a User Coordinate System

We are now ready to apply the roof tile hatching but before hatching we must change the drawing planes to coincide with the roof pitches.

To move the drawing plane to coincide with the roof we will use the **UCS/3Point** command which repositions the X,Y and Z directions.

- From the **View/Toolbars** pull-down menu load the **UCS** toolbar.
- Pick the **UCS 3point** option and the command line will prompt

Command: _ucs

*Current ucs name: *WORLD**

Enter an option [New/Move/orthoGraphic/Prev/Restore/Save/Del/Apply/?/World] <World>: _3

Specify new origin point <0,0,0>: *_int of* ***pick*** *as shown in Figure 9.9*

Specify point on positive portion of X-axis <1.0000,0.0000,0.0000>: *int of* ***pick*** *as shown in Fig. 9.9*

Specify point on positive-Y portion of the UCS XY plane <0.0000,1.0000,0.0000>: *_int of* ***pick*** *as shown in Figure 9.9*

Your drawing should now look like Figure 9.9.

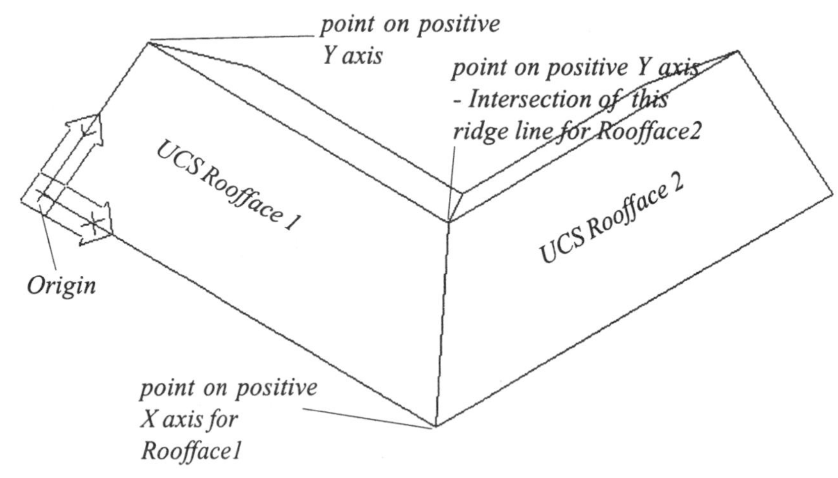

***Figure 9.9**. The new UCS position*

- If the **UCS** icon is not positioned over the new origin, type **UCSicon** at the command line and enter the **Or** for **Origin** option which will place the icon at the new origin as shown in Figure 9.9.

Saving the UCS Position

It is a good idea to save this new drawing plane position by picking the **UCS** button and at the command line type **S** for **Save** with the name **Roofface1**.

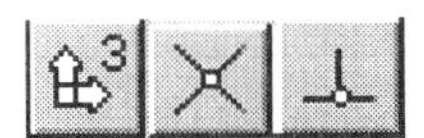

- For **Roofface2** repeat the process of defining the roof plane as before but with the positive portion on the **Y** axis being the **Intersection** of the ridge lines as shown in the construction of **Roofface2** in Figure 9.9.

- Use **UCS/Save** to save the position with the names **Roofface2**.

- Change the view of the drawing by picking the **NW Isometric** button.
- Repeat the process of creating the drawing planes for **Roofface3** and **Roofface4** as shown in Figure 9.10.
- When you define the **UCS** for **Roofface4** the positive portion on the **Y** axis is **Perpendicular** to the ridge as shown in Figure 9.10.

- Save each **UCS** position with the names **Roofface3** and **Roofface4**.

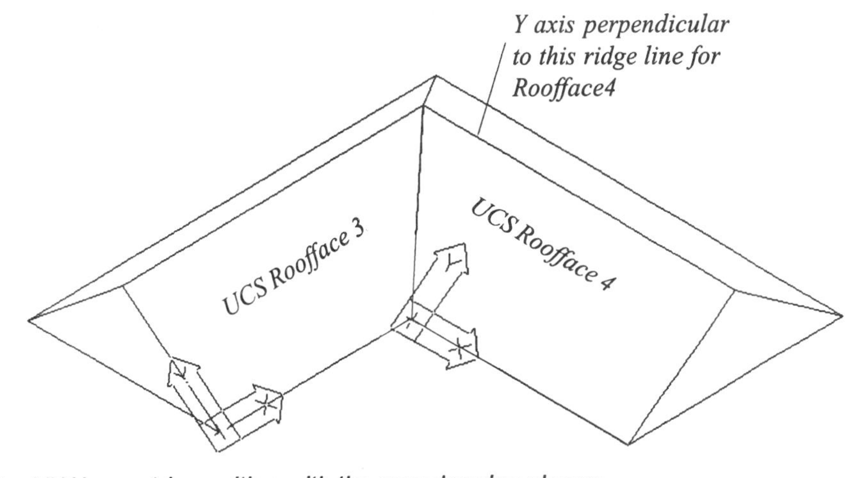

***Figure 9.10**. The NW Isometric position with the new drawing planes*

Changing the UCS

Once you have created a **UCS** you will need to alternate between them. In readiness for hatching the roof we will reinstate **UCS Roofface1**.

Firstly, we will change the view of the drawing.

- Pick the **SE Isometric** button.

- Pick the **Named UCS** button and the **UCS** dialogue box will appear as shown in Figure 9.11.
- Click on **Roofface1** and **Set Current**.
- Click on **OK**.

Roofface1 is now the current **UCS** and the **UCS** icon should be placed at its origin position as shown in Figure 9.9.

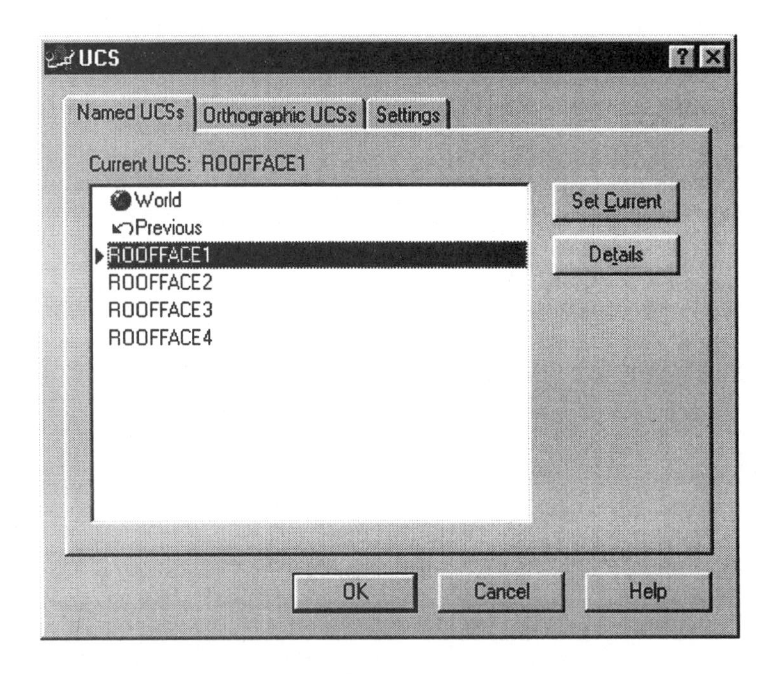

Figure 9.11. The UCS Control dialogue box.

Hatching the Roof

- Thaw the **Roofhatch** layer and make it **Current**.

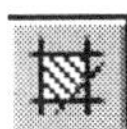

- Pick the **Draw/Hatch** button and the **Boundary Hatch** dialogue box will appear as shown in Figure 9.12.
- Click on the **Pattern** scroll-down arrow.
- Select the **AR-B88** style.
- Click on **Pick Points** and the dialogue box disappears and the command line will prompt

*Command: **_bhatch***

Select internal point: Selecting everything... ***click*** *within the roof boundary*

Selecting everything visible...

Analyzing the selected data...

Analyzing internal islands...

Select internal point: ***Enter***

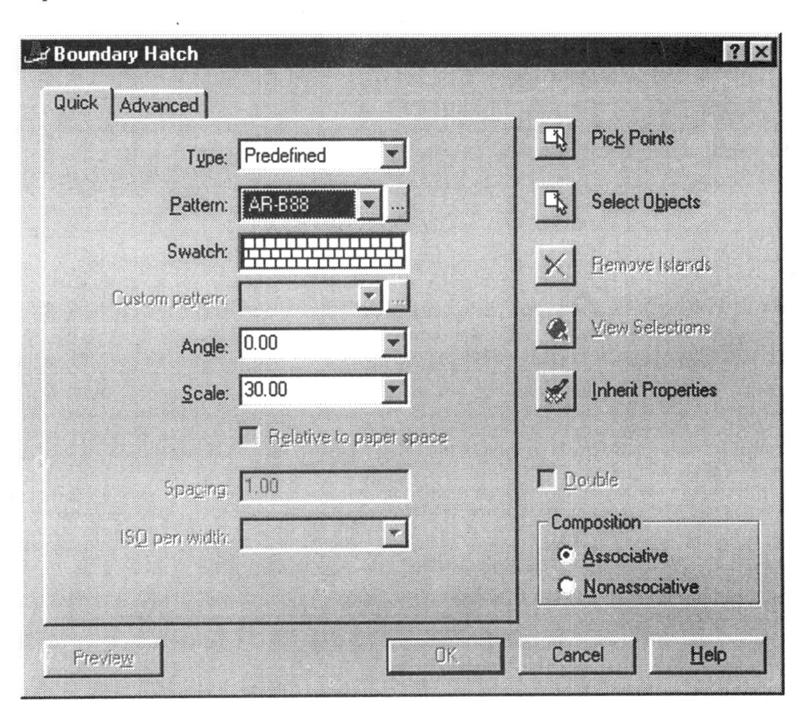

***Figure 9.12**. The Hatch Pattern pallette with AR-B88 selected.*

- You can now either look at the hatch pattern in situ with **Preview** or you can **OK** the pattern. **Preview** gives the opportunity to change the pattern and scale for example before finally clicking on **OK**.

- Change the **Scale** to anything between 30 and 50 for a more or less dense pattern.
- If clicking on **Pick Points** gives a **'Valid hatch boundary not found'** message, use the **Select bjects** button to pick the roof outline.

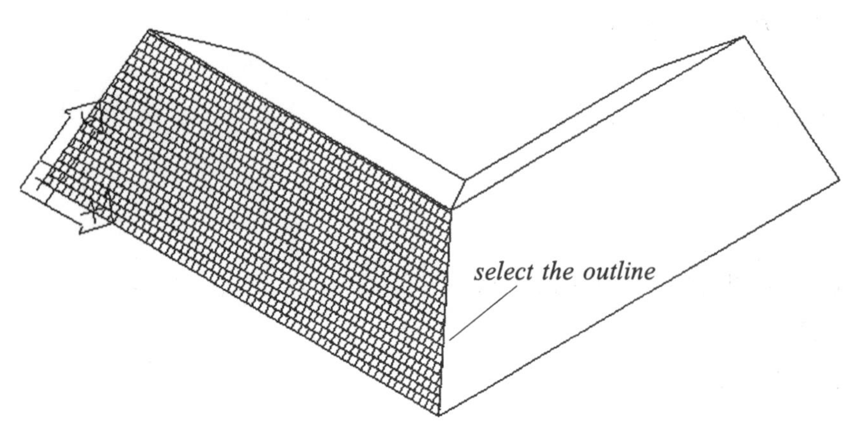

Figure 9.13. *Roofface1 hatched*

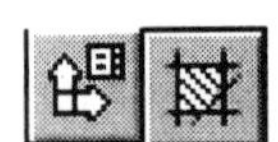

- Restore **UCS Roofface2**.
- **Hatch** that plane as shown in Figure 9.14.

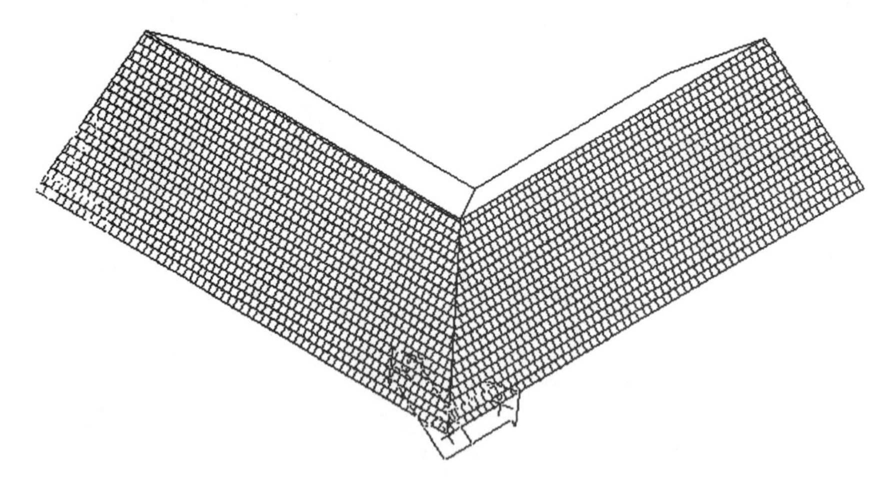

Figure 9.14. *Roofface2 hatched.*

- Pick the **NW Isometric** button.
- Select the **Named UCS** button.
- Restore **UCS Roofface3** and **Hatch** that plane.
- Restore **UCS Roofface4** and finally, hatch that plane.

The drawing should now look Figure 9.15.

- Select the **Named UCS** button and in the **UCS** dialogue box click on **World** and **Set Current**.
- Click on **OK**.
- Close the **UCS** toolbar.

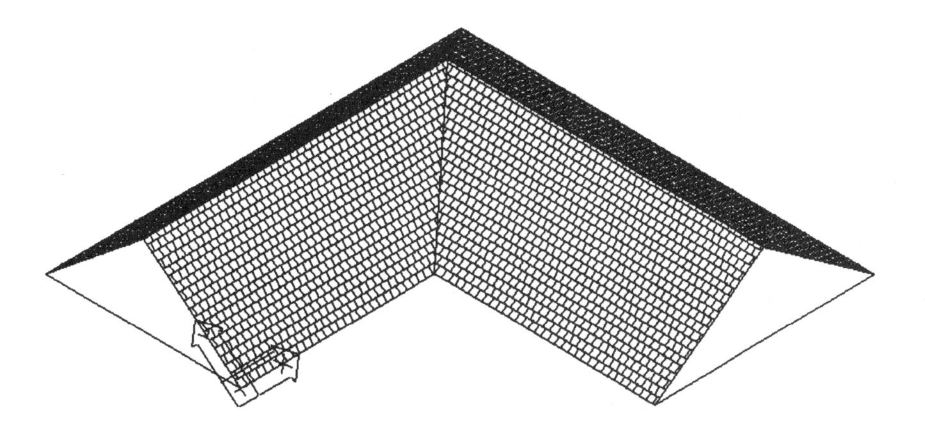

Figure 9.15. *The completed roof hatching*

- **Thaw** all the layers except **Doors, Dimension, Text** and **Furniture**.
- Make layer **0 Current**.
- Use the **Hide** command and the drawing should look like Figure 9.16.

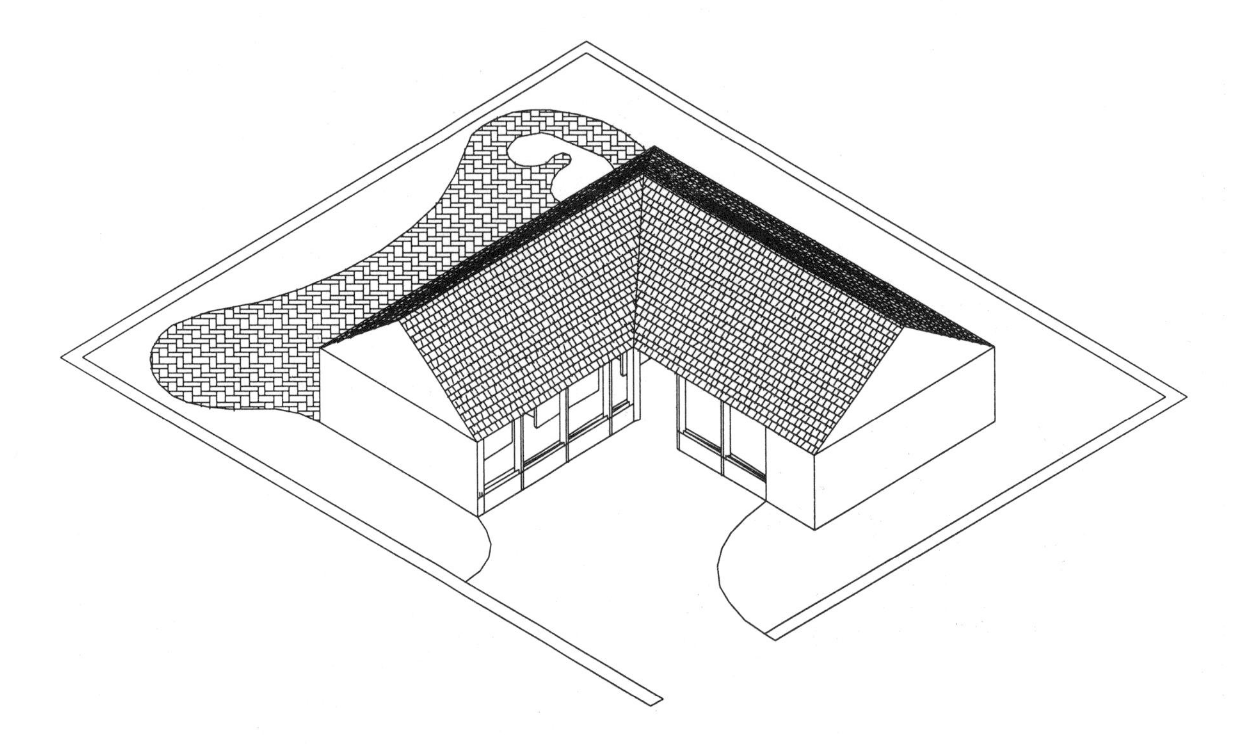

***Figure 9.16**. The completed building looking from the NW Isometric*

To View the Completed 2D target Drawing

- From the **View** pull-down menu select **3DViews/Plan View/World UCS.**
- **Freeze** the **Roof, Rooftile** and **3Dface** layers.
- **Thaw** the **Doors** and **Furniture** layers and the plan view of the drawing should look like Figure 9.17.

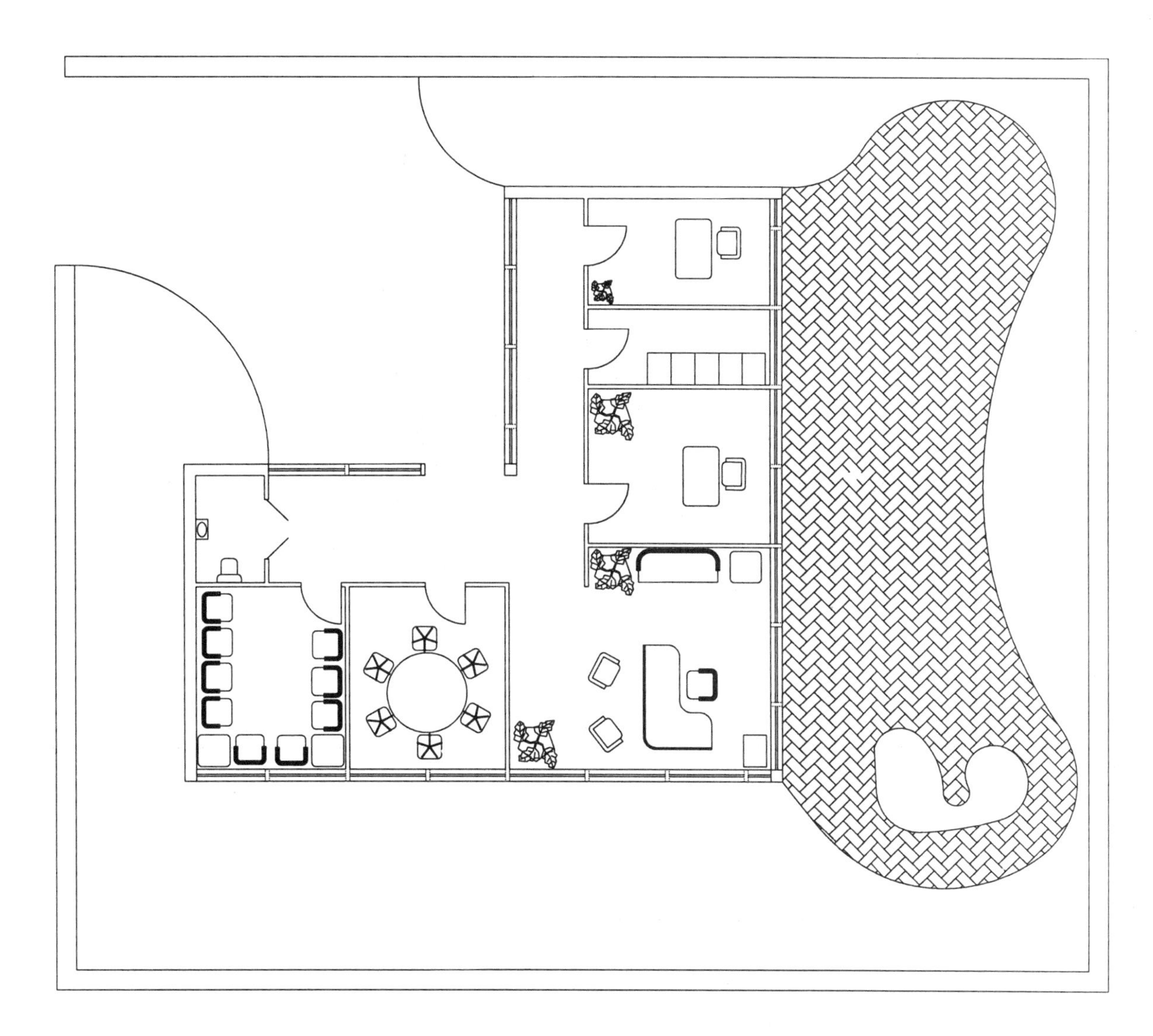

***Figure 9.17**. The completed plan of the building*

Chapter 10 — Paper Space and Plotting

We have completed our drawing in what is known as **Model Space.**

If several tiled viewports are displayed, editing in one viewport affects all other viewports. (We have only used one viewport throughout the drawing). However, you can set magnification, viewpoint, grid, and snap settings individually for each viewport.

The first time you switch to **Paper Space,** the graphics area displays a blank space that represents the "paper" on which you arrange your drawing. In this space, you create **floating viewports** to contain different views of your model as shown in Figure 10.1.

In **Paper Space,** floating viewports are treated as objects that you can move and resize in order to create a suitable layout. You are not restricted to plotting a single **Model Space** view, as you are with **tiled viewports.** Therefore, any arrangement of floating viewports can be plotted. In **Paper Space,** you can also draw objects, such as title blocks or annotations, directly in the **Paper Space** view without affecting the model itself.

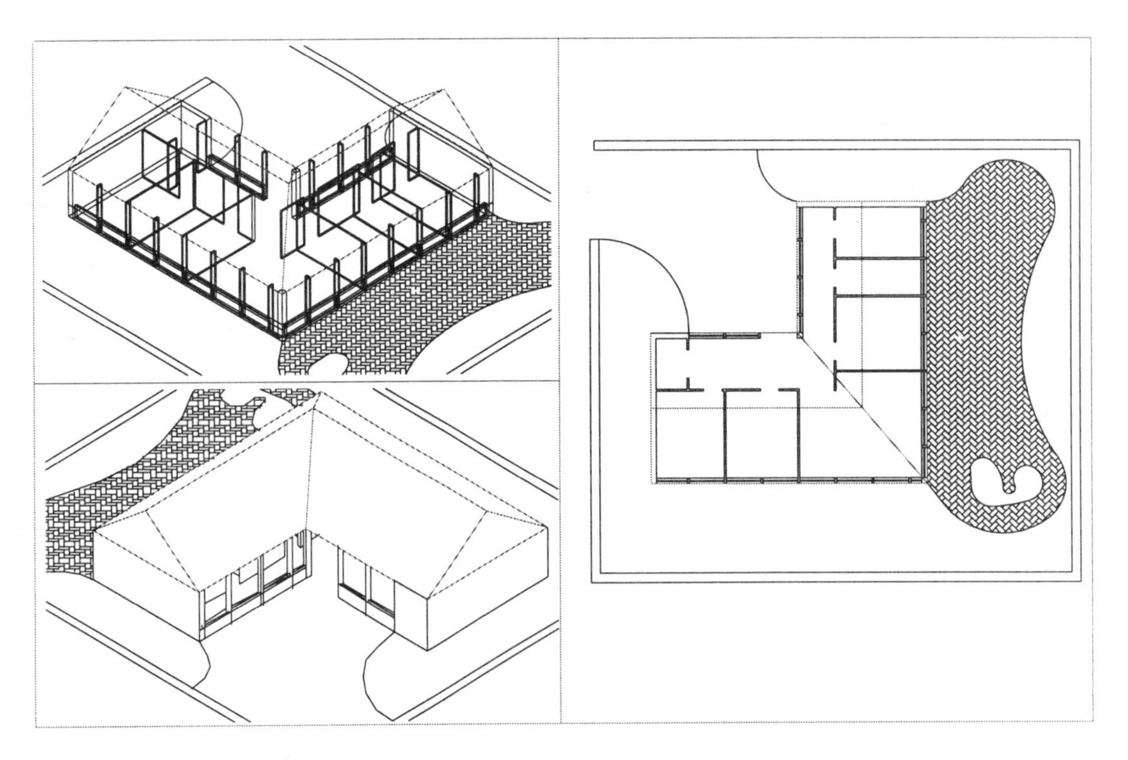

Figure 10.1. *3 different views of the building on one drawing shown with floating viewports*

Model Space and **Paper Space** differ in that **Paper Space** accepts values at a 1:1 ratio so that if you wanted the title of the drawing to be in 10mm high text, in **Paper Space** you would select 10mm high text. In **Model Space** the text height would have to be a multiple of the final plotted scale of the drawing e.g. 10mm high text at scale of 1:50 would be entered at a size of 10x50 = 500mm. When you plot from **Paper Space** the scale is 1:1.

AutoCAD allows us to set up a pre-drawn border in **Paper Space** using the **Use a Wizard/Advanced Setup** facility when a **New** drawing is started. We have not approached drawing in this way, so we will **Insert** the pre-drawn border in **Paper Space**, complete the border drawing information such as the titling and create 3 floating viewports showing different views as shown in Figure 10.2.

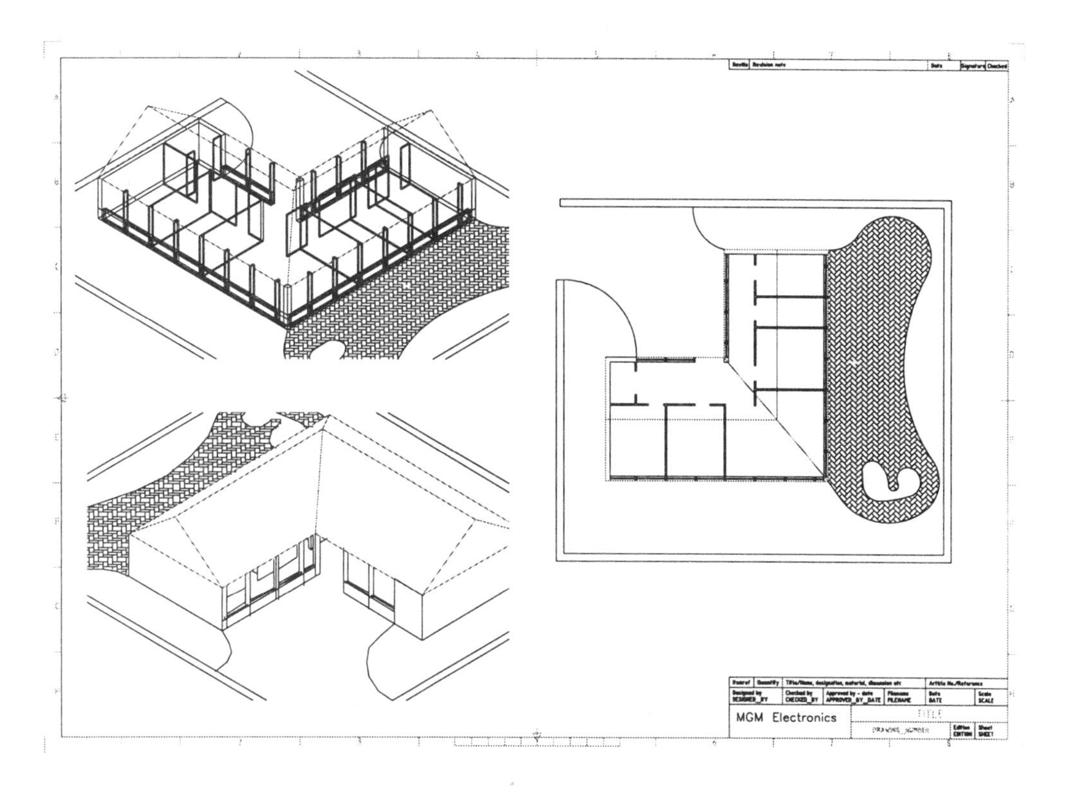

Figure 10.2. *The completed drawing in Paper Space with inserted pre-drawn border and details with viewport boundaries frozen.*

Changing to Paper Space

- To change to **Paper Space** click the **Model** button on the **Status bar** as shown in Figure 10.3.

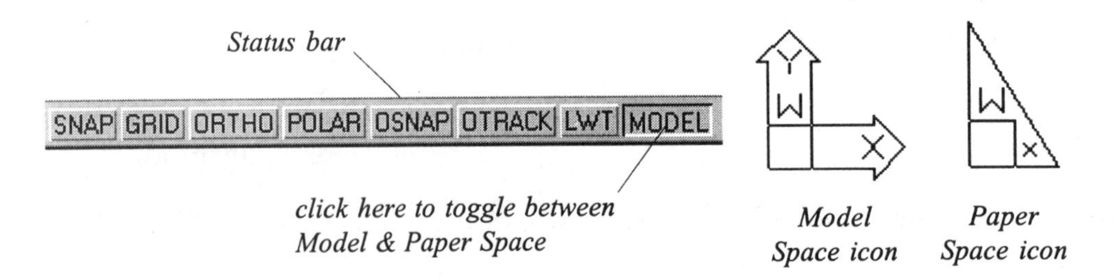

Figure 10.3. The Model Space & Tile toggle buttons with the Paper Space and Model Space icons

- The drawing will disappear leaving a blank screen.
- The **Paper Space** icon appears in the bottom left corner and **Paper** shows on the **Status bar** in place of **Model**.
- The first time you change to **Paper Space** the **Page Setup** dialogue box appears where you set up the plotter type, paper size etc.
- Click on **OK**.
- To return to **Model Space** click on **Paper** at any time.

Inserting the Pre-drawn Border

- Ensure that you are in **Paper Space.**

- Create a layer called **Border**.
- Make **Border** the **Current** layer.

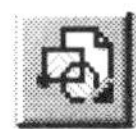

- From the **Insert** pull-down menu pick **Block** and the **Insert** dialogue box will appear asshown in Figure 10.4. We have used this previously when inserting our Furniture blocks.
- Click on **Browse** to access drawings which are independent of our Office drawing.

We are looking for a drawing called **ISO A2 title block.dwg** which you should find in the **Template** folder of AutoCAD.

- Once selected, its name along with its location in the computer appears in the **Name** bar as shown in Figure 10.4.
- Uncheck **Specify on Screen** so that the insertion point of the drawing becomes preset at 0,0,0.

- Place a check in the **Explode** button so that the drawing will appear as separate objects as shown in Figure 10.4.
- Click on **OK**.

We are exploding the drawing so that we can edit the title box of **ISO A2 title block.dwg**. The pre-drawn border now appears on the screen in **Paper Space**.

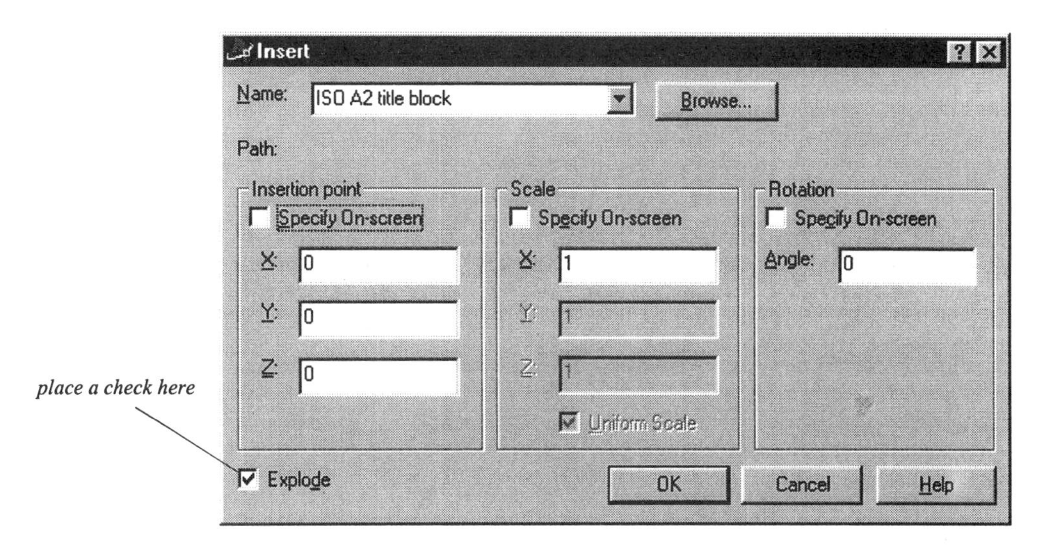

Figure 10.4. *The Insert dialogue box.*

- Use **Zoom/Window** to enlarge the title box area as shown in Figure 10.5.
- **Erase** the word '**Owner**'.

- Create a new layer called **PStext** and make it **Current.**
- From the pull-down menu **Draw/Text** select **Single Line Text** and the command line will prompt

Command: *_dtext*

Current text style: "Standard" Text height: *2.5000*

Specify start point of text or [Justify/Style]: ***j***

Enter an option [Align/Fit/Center/Middle/Right/TL/TC/TR/ML/MC/MR/BL/BC/BR]: ***c (for Centre)***

Specify center point of text: ***pick** the centre of the box as shown in Figure 10.5*

Specify height <2.5000>: ***5** Enter*

Specify rotation angle of text <0>: ***Enter***

Enter text: ***MGM Electronics** Enter*

Enter text: ***Enter***

and the words MGM Electronics will appear as shown in Figure 10.5.

Change other details by **Erasing** '**Designed_By**' and entering your intitials etc into the other boxes. You will need to reduce the text size to suit.

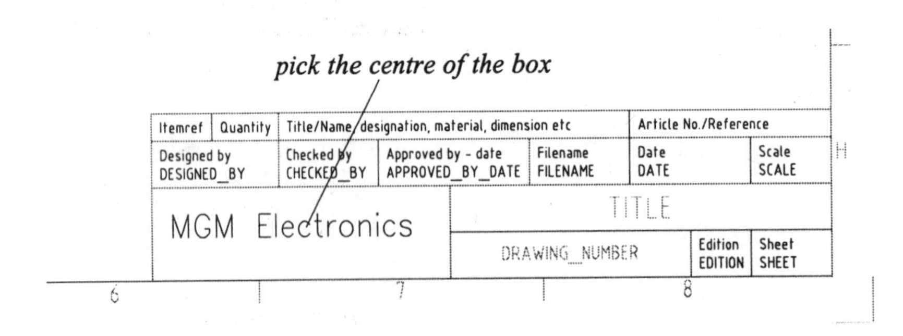

Figure 10.5. The title box of the Inserted ISO_a2 title block drawing

- **Zoom Out** so that all of the border drawing is visible.

- Create a new layer called **PSvports** and make it **Current** with a prominent colour.
- From the pull-down menu **View/Viewports** select **3 Viewports** and the command line will prompt

  Command: _-vports

  Specify corner of viewport or [ON/OFF/Fit/Hideplot/Lock/Object/Polygonal/Restore/2/3/4] <Fit>: _3

  Enter viewport arrangement [Horizontal/Vertical/Above/Below/Left/Right] <Right>: ***Enter***

  Specify first corner or [Fit] <Fit>: ***pick*** *corner as shown in Figure 10.6*

  Specify opposite corner: ***pick*** *corner as shown in Figure 10.6*

  Regenerating model.

The drawing will appear as shown in Figure 10.6 with the same view of the drawing in the 3 viewports.

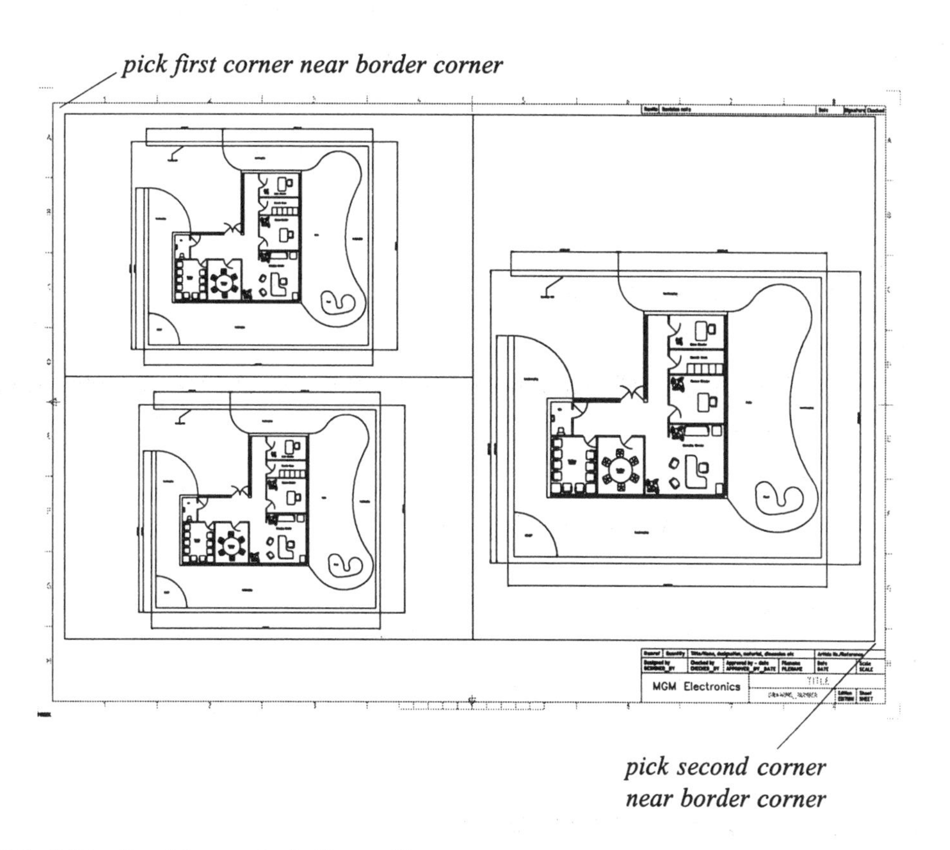

Figure 10.6. *3 Floating Viewports in Paper Space*

Toggling between Model Space and Paper Space

AutoCAD does not allow us to edit the drawing in **Paper Space** so we need to return to **Model Space** to change the views in the left hand viewports.

PAPER

- Click on **Paper** in the **Status bar** and **Model Space** tiled viewports are active.
- Click on the top left viewport to make it the current active viewport.

- Use one of the **Isometric View** buttons to choose a suitable view of your drawing as shown in figure 10.7. You may need to **Zoom** or **Pan** to obtain a view to your liking.

- To **Freeze** layers in the current viewport click on the layer name followed by the **Show Details** button.
- Place a check in the **Freeze in Active Viewports** box.
- Click on **OK**.

Any selected layers will now only be frozen in the currently active viewport.
Repeat the operation for the bottom left viewport to produce a view and visible layers as shown in Figure 10.7.

MODEL

- Click on the **Model button** to return to **Paper Space**.

To view the drawing without viewports visible we need to make another layer **Current** in order to **Freeze** the **PSvports** layer.

- Make layer **0 Current**.
- **Freeze** the **PSvports** layer.

The completed drawing will appear similar to that shown in Figure 10.7 and is now ready for plotting.

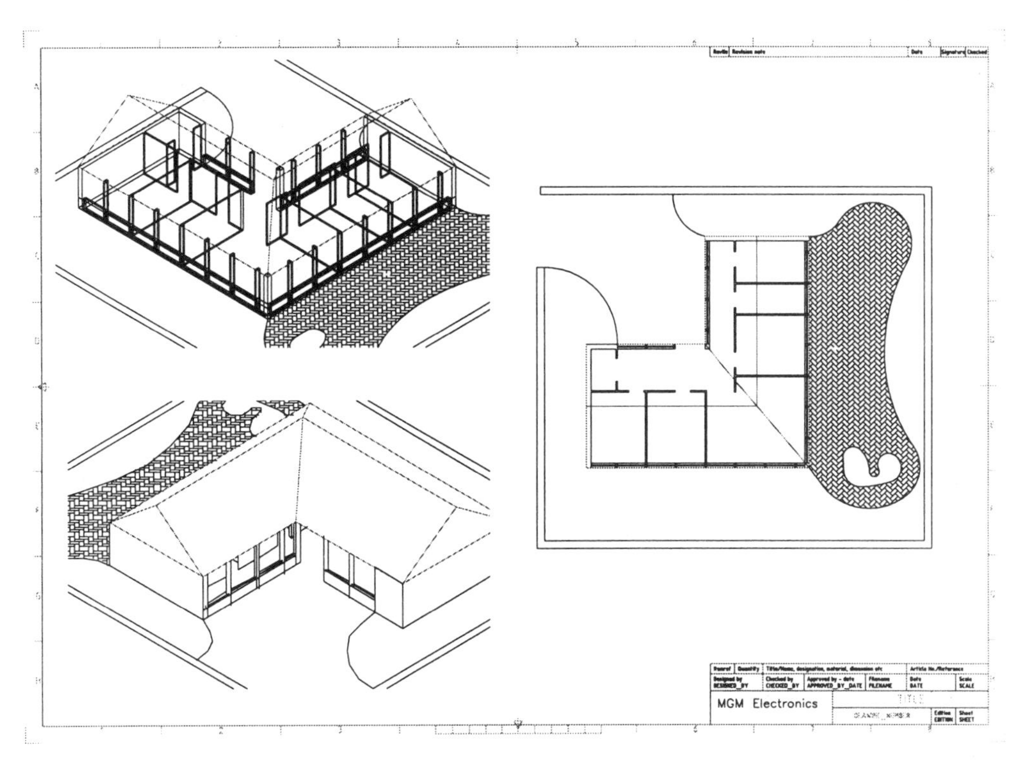

***Figure 10.7**. The completed drawing showing views with viewport boundaries frozen.*

Plotting the Drawing

- Before activating the **Print** command and still in **Paper Space** we must turn **Hideplot** to **On** to prevent the viewport boundaries appearing on the plotted drawing.
- **Thaw** the **Psvports** layer.
- At the command line type **Mview** to select the 3 viewport boundaries.

Command: ***mview***

Specify corner of viewport or [ON/OFF/Fit/Hideplot/Lock/Object/Polygonal/Restore/2/3/4] <Fit>: ***h***

Hidden line removal for plotting [ON/OFF]: ***on***

Select objects: 1 found ***select a viewport boundary***

Select objects: 1 found ***select a viewport boundary***

Select objects: 1 found ***select a viewport boundary***

Select objects: ***Enter***

- **Freeze** the **Psvports** layer.

Assuming a plotter or printer is attached and has been configured,

- Click on the **Print** button.
- A dialogue box appears as shown in Figure 10.8.
- Set a scale of **1=1**.
- Check the **Display** button.
- Place a check also, in the **Hide Objects** box.
- Activate a **Full Preview** to check the plot is correct.
- When you are satisfied, load the plotter or printer with the plotting media.
- Click on **OK** to plot the drawing.

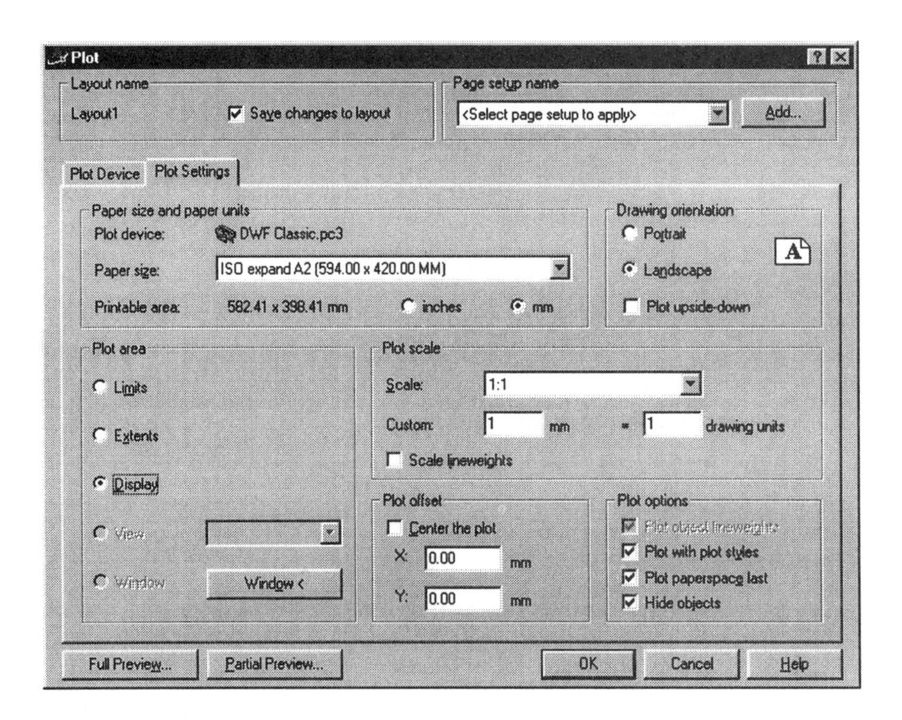

***Figure 10.8**. The Plot dialogue box.*

Introduction

to

AutoCAD 2000

Published by
Payne-Gallway P
78 Christchurch S
Ipswich IP4 2DE
Tel 01473 251
Fax 01473 23
E-mail payne_gall

2000

Acknowledgements

I would like to thank Pat and Oliver Heathcote at Payne-Gallway for their enthusiasm and advice. Grateful thanks to Martin Pacey of Somerset College of Arts & Technology for correcting my AutoCAD mistakes and omissions. Above all, thanks to Monica for her endless patience and understanding.

First edition 2000
A catalogue entry for this book is available from the British Library
ISBN 1 903112 23 0

Printed in Great Britain by
WM Print Ltd, Walsall, West Midlands, England.

Index

Symbols

A

B

C

D

E

F

G

H

I

K

L

M

Ordering information

You can order by phone, fax, post or e-mail from:

BEBC (The Bournemouth English Book Centre)
Albion Close
Parkstone, Poole
Dorset BH12 3LL

Tel: 01202 712934
Fax: 01202 712913
e-mail: pg@bebc.co.uk

Visit our web site at www.payne-gallway.co.uk for news about the latest titles and information about prices.